STATUS AND EMPOWERMENT OF TRIBAL WOMEN IN TRIPURA

STATUS AND EMPOWERMENT OF TRIBAL WOMEN IN TRIPURA

Dr. (Mrs.) Krishna Nath (Bhowmik)

KALPAZ PUBLICATIONS
DELHI - 110 052

Status and Empowerment of Tribal Women in Tripura

Rs. 750

ISBN : 81-7835-289-3

Published in 2005 in India by
Kalpaz Publications,
C-30, Satyawati Nagar,
Delhi-110 052
Email : kalpaz@hotmail.com

Lasertype Setting by: Tact Computer Graphics, Delhi
Printed at: Salasar Imaging System, Delhi

Contents

Contents

Preface

The most current and important topic of today is to review the status of women both on national as well as state level. Fifty-seven years have gone after independence yet women in general and the tribal women in particular are the most neglected, underprivileged and downtrodden section almost in all fields. The women societies in almost all countries are like a lamp that burns itself to lit the whole world yet its own down part is ever sunk in darkness. The tribal world of women is this down part that remained in darkness during centuries after centuries. The year 2001 was declared as the Women's Empowerment Year by the Government of India to combat this century old backwardness. In this regard the present work has been innovated and a little effort on my part to offer my heartfelt empathy towards them is done to make it a tribute in name of them. There are total 19 tribes in Tripura and out of them; I have discussed four major tribes namely, the Tripuri, the Reang, the Jamatia and the Chakma in detail for more than one reason. These four tribes not only in their numerical strength but also in their progress and development almost on every fields in general and women in particular are able to get the fruit of benefits of government schemes. They are followed by five tribes in their numerical strength namely the Halam, the Lushai, the Mog, the Kuki and the Garo who also are brought but here a major obstruction arises to discuss the status & empowerment of their women as women development in particular is not so developed like the formers' and the rest other ten tribes namely the Munda, the Noatia, the

Orang, the Santal, the Uchai, the Khasi, the Bhil, the Lepcha, the Bhutia and the Chaimal can be discussed generally but as my study dealt with the Tribal women in particular, no mentionworthy records of their women development on the field of education or economy or politics leading to their empowerment to secure any stable status are found. If the present trend of consciousness of education among the tribal communities for their girls continues, after one or two decades, the picture will definitely be changed to produce new records to bring forth.

First of all, I must mention the name of my reverend teacher Shri Saroj Kr. Choudhury, retired Vice Principal and a renowned English teacher for about forty years who, in spite of his busy schedule went through my work very minutely and sincerely with suggestions where necessary. Therefore my regards and gratitude know no bound for him.

Next I express my heartfelt thank to Smt. Bithika Deb Barma, Ex-member of Tripura Public Service Commission, previously Deputy Secretary of the Government of Tripura for her hearty cooperation and good wishes regarding this work. My special thank goes to Smt. Manika Talukder, Joint Director, Higher Education, Govt of Tripura and Smt. Karabi Deb Barma, retired Principal, Government Women's College, Agartala for their helpful assistance. I must thank Dr. K.B. Jamatia, Deputy Registrar, Tripura University who also helped me in this regard. I am also grateful to Dr. (Mrs.) Chandrika Bose Majumder, Reader and Head of the Deptartment of Political Science, Tripura University,who deserves my gratitude as she made arrangement for my field work on some tribal women. I must mention the name of Smt. Mithu Ghosh, part time Lecturer, Department of Philosophy, M.B.B.College and Shri Alok Ghosh, journalist of the *Dainik Sambad,* Agartala who helped me by supplying some rare journals. Mr. K.D. Nath, Director of Census, Government of Tripura and Dr. Jagadish Gon Choudhury, Reader, Political Science, B.B. Memorial College, Agartala are the two mentionworthy persons who helped me in many ways. I convey my gratitude to Smt. Kalyani Bhattacherjee, Editor of *Manabi,* a women's magazine for rendering her help in this work. I am also indebted to M.B.B. College Library, the Tribal Research Library, Directorate of Economics and Statistics, Govt. of Tripura as the authorities of these concerns helped me in numerous ways.

Finally, the undescribable, immeasurable and untiring help, co-operation and encouragement of my husband Dr. Dwijendra Lal Bhowmik, Reader and Head of the Department of Philosophy, M.B.B. College, Agartala, made me indebted to him for ever. I must mention the name of my only son, Durjoy Bhowmik who always bears patiently all his mother's engagements and absence with encouragement from his part.

I shall consider my labour rewarded if it is found helpful in any way. In spite of my best efforts, still some typographical errors might have been there which may kindly be considered by the readers.

Agartala, **Dr. (Mrs.) Krishna Nath (Bhowmik).**

The 25 Jan.'2005

1
Introduction

In his novel, *Aranyak,* Bibhuti Bhushan Banerjee wrote in one place that he does not understand why some castes with their inherent hidden seeds of civilization, march much forward towards progress and development with the passage of time, whereas some others remain unmoved and still in one place for thousand of years....and the Mundas, the Koles, the Nagas, the Kukis are those people in India to live at that stagnant position for five hundred years...why? More than 75 years back, Bibhuti Bhushan put these questions before us and with this quest in our mind, the journey has been started to wake up these sections of our society from their slumber. We have just entered into the 21st century with new hope and promise to do much better in bringing these sections into the mainstream of national life and culture.

Though Tripura is a tiny state and formerly was a very small kingdom under Tripura's royal Dynasty, yet its tradition is rich in many ways. We get the proof of it in Rajmala, the chronicle history of Tripura's Royal Dynasties. From this princely state, the modern Tripura is born. From last few decades, many attempts were made to search out and reveal many more hidden authentic historical paradigms to unearth the golden past. To fulfil this aim, already many prudent personalities and erudite scholars with limited sources and almost bleak treasure of evidence brought out fruits which are not only resourceful but also helpful and extremely useful for the coming generation's scholars and interested people who would like to add more gifts to this treasure house.

As a present day scholar and particularly a woman, I noticed one thing very minutely which I think everyone would agree with. Almost all previous scholars and researchers for last two decades dealt with Tripura's histories, presented valuable customs and events of the tribal communities, their dresses, habits, looks and focused on their traditional tales. But the study on the tribal women is an untraversed field still now. This area is yet mostly neglected, almost untouched and untold. Therefore, the need arises that we have to dive deeply to bring out the hidden pearl from its untold cover. So here is an humble attempt to discuss the status and empowerment of the tribal women of Tripura whose history goes back to the Royal Dynasty days and my attempt is to start from there at the root of women emergence.

Keeping this aim in my mind, I started my attempt in different libraries at Agartala and after surveying almost all libraries situated at Agartala's different departments, public libraries, Universities and College libraries, I had the opportunities to go through many different books written by renowned personalities, recording the ascendance of the first Royal Tribal kings, their individual periods of achievements on many fields, the name of other important personalities and dignitaries holding different royal posts etc. but seldom the names of their queens or wives or other female members of family have been recorded side by side with these kings and others. Few names of the queens and other royal ladies that appear also very occasionally and casually. In Government Gazettes also, two or three queens such as the Queen Jhanavi, Queen Kanchanprava, Queen Gunabati etc. are mentioned just by names but not with any individuality. Although it is a fact that the benevolent King Radhakishore Manikya opened a girls' school at Agartala which he named after his Queen Maharani Tulsibati where the girls of Tripura first got the chance to study. In this way I try my best to accumulate those sporadic paradigms of little mentioned or almost not mentioned women folk to show the social, economic, educational condition of women not only of that two centuries back but also up to the present days.

The tribal women of the 21st Century pose more daring, self conscious and outspoken. Literacy has lit of every good thing in the life of tribal women. But this literacy rate is high mostly in Agartala and the places closer to it. The remote hill areas are still lagging far behind in literacy particularly for the tribal women. Some Christian missionary schools in these areas are imparting education among the tribals allegedly on conversion ground but here also the boys got much more advantages than girls as boys could be sent abroad to take the proper training and then come back to serve for their religion. So here also, the percentage of literacy among tribal women is extremely low.

The tribal society is also a patriarchal society and so the dominance of male members over the female members is obvious. And it is a burning truth that no country in the world treats its women as well as its men. It is also well known that there cannot be any educated people without educated women. This is the reason that every opportunity should be given to women, as it would most surely be passed on to the next generation. And without education, political and economic empowerment for assuming a desired status in development would be distant goals.

But what does empowerment actually mean? It can be defined simply that empowerment means the ability to change everything one desires. Women's empowerment means women's ability and control over resources and the power to take decisions on all major issues concerning their lives. So access to knowledge on issues like education, health, legal rights, technological innovations are just some of the factors that help in developing the potential of an individual by creating a level of confidence and self image that further generates a desire to achieve greater control and participation in the decision making process. But this empowerment becomes impossible without proper education. Centuries after centuries, women suffer exploitation, negligence and apathy, which strangle the spirit of them. Nature also handicapped women by creating them physically weak and by giving them the pain to bear the burden of procreation, which definitely chain women into universal helplessness. In addition to these unprecedented weakness, women are denied all privileges which the male world enjoys so freely and merrily. Again by nature, women are gifted with the power of endurance and tolerance. Their mental strength is much higher than their physical strength and so traditionally women silently bear all traumas, tortures, violence, maladjustment and still today, they are the mute persons subject to male's whims very easily. That is why, today's women need total empathy rather than damp and foolish sympathy to stand erect in male dominated bastion.

So to discuss the status and empowerment of women and that also of the tribal women is not only a very tough task but the result is also very bleak, whenever the forward classes of women still don't find their footings as desired, achievements of the tribal women in mass find it more hard and troublesome. The total progress of the tribal women of Tripura is extremely slow still today. In this respect, both the tribal men and women are more or less advanced equally particularly in urban areas. Of course in the last decade, the development of the tribal women specially on education level for pursuing a good career is quite evident and this awareness is equally emerging both in rural and urban levels.

As to the number of tribes of present Tripura, the Government of India Notification of 1956 declares that there are 19 (nineteen) Scheduled Tribes here. (*Source:* Tripura District- Gazetteers, p.143 Edited by K.D. Menon, Agartala, 1975, also Government of Tripura - Statistical Dept. Instructions for filling up the Returns on Annual Census of Employees, p. 8). They are in order of numerical strength:Tripura, (or Tripuri or Tippera) Reang, Jamatia, Chakma, Halam, Noatia, Mog, Kuki, Garo, Munda, Lusai, Orang, Santal, Uchai, Khasi, Bhil, Lepcha, Bhutia and Chaimal. In addition with this, some think that, there is a tribe called Desi Tripura, some reckon several of these tribes (Jamatia, Reang, Noatia etc.,) as branches of the Tripuri tribe, because they speak dialects of the Tripuri or Kokborok language.

The comparative numerical strength of the 19th tribes is shown in the following table as per census reports:

Table 1

Tribe Wise Population of Tripura at a Glance (1931-2001) Census

Sl. No.	*Name of the Tribe*	*1931*	*1951*	*1961*	*1971*	*1981*	*1991*	*2001*
1.	Bhil	-	41	69	169	838	Total S.T. 8,53,345, 30.95% of the Total population. Tribewise Population not available.	2336
2.	Bhutia	-	19	7	3	22		29
3.	Chaimal	-	220	50	-	18		226
4.	Chakma	8730	7277	22386	28662	34797		64293
5.	Garoo	2144	7352	5484	5559	7297		11180
6.	Halam	12713	1644	16296	19076	28969		47245
7.	Jamatia	11090	2764	24359	34192	44501		74949
8.	Khasia	-	151	349	491	457		630
9.	Kuki	1479	2721	5531	7775	5501		11674
10.	Lepcha	-	5	7	14	106		105
11.	Lushai	2175	1947	2988	3672	3734		4777

(Contd...)

(Contd...)

Sl. No.	*Name of the Tribe*	*1931*	*1951*	*1961*	*1971*	*1981*	*1991*	*2001*
12.	Mag	5748	3789	10524	13273	181231	Census Report of S.T. 2001 not yet Published.	30385
13.	Munda, Kaur	2058	51	4409	5347	7993		12416
14.	Noatia	27405	1916	16010	10297	7182		6655
15.	Orang	979	-	2875	3428	5271		6223
16.	Riang	25881	8471	56597	64722	84003		165103
17.	Santal	735	736	1562	2222	2726		2151
18.	Tripuri Tripura	79074	150971	189799	250545	330872		543848
19.	Uchai	-	-	766	1061	1306		2103
	Unspecified	-	2218	-	36	-		7098
	Total	**190211**	**192293**	**360070**	**450544**	**583700**		**993426**

Table 2
Tribewise Population of Tripura

Sl. No.	*Name of the Tribe*	*Census Years*			
		1971	*1981*	*1991*	*2001*
1.	Bhil	169	838	1754	2336
2.	Bhutia	3	22	47	29
3.	Chaimal	0	18	26	226
4.	Chakma	28662	34797	96096	64293
5.	Garoo	5559	7297	9360	11180
6.	Halam	19076	28969	36499	47245
7.	Jamatia	34192	44501	60824	74949
8.	Khasia	491	457	358	630
9.	Kuki	7775	5501	10628	11674
10.	Lepcha	14	106	111	105
11.	Lushai	3672	3734	4910	4777
12.	Mag	13273	18231	31612	30385

(Contd...)

(Contd...)

Sl. No.	Name of the Tribe	Census Years			
		1971	1981	1991	2001
13.	Munda, Kaur	5347	7993	11547	12416
14.	Noatia	10297	7182	4158	6655
15.	Orang	3428	5217	6751	6223
16.	Reing	64722	84003	111606	165103
17.	Santal	2222	2726	2736	2151
18.	Tripuri Tripura	250545	330872	461531	543848
19.	Uchai	1061	1306	1637	2103
20	Generic Tribes	-	-	-	7098
	Total	**450508**	**583770**	***853345**	**993426**

* Total Scheduled Tribes includes figures for unclassified.

References

Census Birbarani of 1931, Tripura, Samarendra Chandra Deb Barma, Census Office.

District Census Hand Book of 1951, Tripura.

Census of India, 1961, Tripura, Superintendent of Census Operation, Tripura.

Census of India, 1971 Tripura, Director of Census Operation, Tripura.

Census of India, 1981 Tripura, Director of Census Operation, Tripura.

2

A Glimpse of the Tribal Women in Royal Families

In vedic era of ancient India, there are numerous example in which it is clearly evident that women were quite learned and imparted their acquired rich knowledge to their offspring. A well educated woman with good knowledge only can become an ideal mother and an ideal wife and this concept was not created in one day but had been reflected and established in different sermons of the Vedas and the Upanishads. Biswabara, Ghosa, Romza were some ancient women of India who were highly regarded for their excellent wisdom and knowledge. Their philosophical excellence made the ancient sages so impressed that they worshipped women as goddess of learning. The two other extremely learned Aryan women, Maitreyee and Gargee studied and cultured Sanskrit and anthology with Jagyavalkya, the most learned saint of ancient India. Leelabati was another lady who was extremely proficient in math. The daughter of king Rajyabardhan of Thaneswar Kingdom, Rajyasree was extremely talented in dance and song. In our two Indian epics, the Ramayana and the Mahavarata, we get evidence of freedom for women who got the right to choose their own life partners. The ready wit of Draupadi, the farewell speech,full of depth and knowledge of Sita, the Queen Madalasa's teaching of knowledge of Absolute proved that ancient women of India were quite learned and self confident. Of course, the number of these women was countable who belonged to the upper strata of the society.

With the passage of time, this golden past of restricted learning for women of upper class is gradually downtrodden by numerous foreign invaders who ruled and moulded their kingdom according to their whims and wills. The most affected section was women whose freedom and education were restricted and later denied to enchain them into the four walls. The history of the world shows that women, almost half of the total population got victim of deprivation in almost all fields just on their gender base.

The fact that the women were looked down upon as something sub human and sometimes even evil, is borne out by many scriptural texts written by men for their own benefits. In Vedic period, Manusmriti was a moral code of law on Hindu marriage, divorce, inheritance, sale, debts etc. in which women were described as false, a misfortune, passion like wine or chess. For killing a blackbird, mongoose, rat, dog, sudra and a woman, the same rite is prescribed. Thus time and again, the women, even if she is endowed with every quality, is inferior to a worthless man.

So it is not very easy to make men respect women's work and talent as they are quite disdainful about these qualities in women. The more talented woman brings more resentment in man. He never loses an opportunity to blow out of all proportions the least in him and is extremely vocal about that but the same talent goes unnoticed in a woman.

Thus, in a male dominated world women accepted and rationalized their plight with compromise on every field. From our epics and mythologies, numerous examples can be cited where male dominance and injustice are quietly accepted by women without a murmur. Sita in the Ramayana was put into ordeals by her very beloved husband Ram. She was sent to banishment with her advanced pregnancy to enhance her husband's prestige. After she proved herself 'pure', being encouraged by watching a washer man charge his wife of adultery, again Ram urges his wife Sita to go through an *Agnipareeksha.* Sita, her head suitably bowed, agrees for it is her husband who has asked her to demonstrate her purity.

In the Mahabharata, Draupadi had to accept all the Pandava brothers as her husbands though she was won only by Arjuna in Swayambara Sabha, whether she obeyed the decision willingly or unwillingly had not been recorded in the story but it is the fact that a very clever diplomatic device had been played by the Pandavas to regain their lost kingdom and power in that way.

Indra, the rain god, mesmerized by the beauty of Ahalya, the wife of the sage Gautama can no longer control his lust for her. He disguises himself as her husband by the power of magic, to take the full advantage without any hindrance. The sage by his supernatural power realizes everything and suitably enraged. But instead of giving any support and protection to his innocent wife, he curses Ahalya by turning her into a stone and lets Indra, the true culprit and the dirty sinner, get scot free as he commits a common male act,a mere peccadillo. Whereas the poor Ahalya accepts this punishment as her unprecedented fate, her usual female destiny.

Thus, most epics and myths look at women as *devis* as long as they obey their master, the lord Parameshwar, husband. As the pen is in the hands of the men, they revolve history and philosophy around them and dictate rules and regulations in scriptures beneficial for themselves. Thus a man can marry as many times as he wants, demands and commands all properties, all good things, all happiness, dictates a masterly attitude on everything.

Women on the other hand is hardly considered a human being, has no right to wealth or over her own body or mind. So the curse of widowhood happens for her own sin as a result of her own ominous misfortune. Adultery is gladly permissible to men for their superior gender whereas women accept this adultery of men by serving them as 'Sevadasi'. A man marries within the seven days of his wife's death as he cannot control his lust and sexual urge but a woman after her husband's death cannot marry as she is 'Devi' and if she desires to marry, she is an 'Evil',she is a woman of bad character. Again a widow is never allowed to enter any social rituals, specially the auspicious ones. Thus time and again, the scriptures say that woman is inherently evil, and so women can be easily stoned to death or stripped to parade nakedly in front of whole village or can easily be defined as 'witch' if she raises any voice against the violence done on her.

In our oriental culture, the general conception regarding women is completely paradoxical. On the one hand women were looked down upon as something false and on the other hand, she is worshipped as 'Devi' - a mysterious enigma. The goddess of strength is Durga, Kali, the goddess of wealth is Laxmi, the goddess of learning is Saraswati, the most pious river of the Hindu is Ganga and numerous other examples are there about women god. At the same time women are treated as inanimate objects, whether in domestic front or in outer world, violence against them is a common feature still today. Often men behave better with animals than with their women.

But as the tribal people almost all communities of Tripura are basically much more simple minded and of down to earth frame of spirit, female world is less prone to exploitation, violence and discrimination. It is unthinkable, that so called atrocities to the female can be attributed in the tribal communities also. According to

Dr. Suchinta Bhattacharjee, "The position of the married women in the household is also changed considerably. Previously a tribal woman enjoyed sufficient liberty in regard to domestic works, marital separation, visits to the parents house etc. But now-a-days, she has been reduced to a subordinate position under the complete authoritative domination of her husband as in a Bengali family".(Genesis of tribal Extremism in Tripura.)

The same point has been cited also by R.H. Sneyd Hutchinson in Chittagong Hill Tracks. Young girls lead an entirely unrestricted life before matrimony, and in the event of pregnancy matrimony follows as a general rule. Should the man refuse to make amends by marriage, he is fined thirty rupees and a pig. The latter provides a feast for the village elders who have decided the case. Unchastity after marriage is comparatively rare. Widows are allowed to remarry and no restriction is placed on their selection. Though the plebian tribal women are much more free who don't bother for any 'veil' or 'parda', the royal tribal women were denied this freedom as the curtain system was in existence strictly for them. The aristocrate tribal women of Royal family never came outside without any veil. In Udaipur, when these ladies went to visit the temple of Tripura Sundari, the employees held up long cloth at the two sides of the road to hide them from the common people. These royal ladies also enjoyed different theatre, jatras etc. behind the curtain.

In Royal Dynasties of Tripura, polygamy is permitted for the kings as well for men of rich background as they alone can afford the luxury of paying for and supporting a plurality of wives. So most of the Tribal kings keep more than one wife. *The Rajmala,* a verse chronicle of the Royal house records this important social event for many kings. The King Uday Manikya had 240 wives. The King Kashichandra and the King Krishnakishore married many Manipuri girls, though most of the names were recorded nowhere. The King Ishan Chandra, the King Birchandra, the King Radha Kishore, the King Birendra Kishore and the King Bir Bikram were all polygamous Kings of Tripura. In the same way the royal ministers and the royal generals and the high officials were also not lagging far behind in practicing polygamy.

It is a fact that the result of this polygamy system ushered in ill consequenced effect on society and family yet the kings and the wealthy tribal aristocrates of Tripura never got rid of it. Though the numbers of these queens and women were given some times fictitiously in different books but some authentic records are also found. The proof that Kalyan Manikya had three wives is found in *'Shrenimala'* book. It was also said that the kings of that time did not bother at all for keeping unnumbered wives. Shri K.P. Sen in his *Rajmala* Part-III, pp. 155-157 counted the wives of some kings with the number 'budi' which denotes that five gandas make one "budi'.

But though the women in all tribal communities are much more free as far as marriage is concerned; in selecting of partner, restriction in married life or to get divorce are much more liberal, yet marriage is 'to be all and end all' for tribal women also. This is reason, more probably, that polygamy is completely nonexistent in tribal women's life. That is why it is found that many tribal queens and tribal ladies of that status embrace 'Sati' rather than marry for second or third time though it was the customary law for the tribal women that a widow could marry again. So though widow marriage is almost permissible in tribal women's lives, it is unthinkable that a tribal queen gets more than one husband.

Tripura's history shows that many queens become 'Sati' the custom which was actually prevalent in Hindu society at that time. Actually it was in the Muslim era that the Hindu women were often at the center of extreme oppression by the Muslim youths and to save the Hindu women from their torture and shame, the child marriage was introduced. And so it happens that the bride was merely a child whose husband was three to four times elder than her and mostly she had to face widowhood. Naturally the young widow wife prefers to become 'Sati' at her husband's pyre. A brief description of some of the magnanimous tribal women of the royal background at that time whose name have been mentioned occasionally in the *Rajmala* is given below:

Queen Kamalabati

When the king Dhanya Manikya (1490-1515) died of small pox, his Queen Kamalabati became sati on his pyre. The Queen Kamalabati always inspired the king to dig ponds to help the poor from the scarcity of water. She was also an ardent lover of language and literature like the king. Some Sanskit texts named Utkalakhanda, the Jatra named Ratnakar Bidhi, Pret Chaturdashi etc. were translated into Bengali by her encouragement.

Queen Jaya

There is also the references to other tribal 'Sati' queens who were extremely benevolent and soft hearted towards their subjects. In the first part of Tripuri by Birendranath Bhatterjee, it was written that Uday Manikya's daughter queen Jaya also wanted to die in her husband's pyre but could not do it for her father's resistance. Jaya's father Gopi Prasad was senapati of Anantya Manikya, son of Bijoy Manikya and after the marriage of his daughter Jaya with Anantya Manikya, Gopi Prasad got tempted by the throne, secretly murdered his son-in-law. The Queen Jaya came to know the fact and scolded her criminal father and jumped on her husband's pyre. Her father's timely intervention saved her from an untimely death and later she ascended the throne.

Queen Jahnnavi Devi

Queen Jahnnavi Devi whose another name was Rani Champa, was extremely prudent with a golden heart. When the King Krishna Manikya died in 1783, the Queen Jahnnavi Devi wanted to become a sati. But a quarrel broke out over succession. So to save the kingdom from the foreigners who were in nexus with inter family relations, the queen had to leave the idea of Sati and instead took the control over the kingdom. The queen and the king were issueless. There were mainly two claimants for the throne, Rajdhar Manikya, the nephew of the late king and Durgamani, the son of Lakshman Manikya. To avoid civil war, Queen Jahannavi Devi took the administration into her own hand and ruled for more than two years (1783-85). In the mean time, she made a petition to the English Government for final arrangement.

During her short reign, she gave ample proof of her ability as a sound administrator. She excavated the Ranir Dighi in Comilla, now in Bangladesh and built the Radha Madhava Temple at Radhanagar. She was also proficient in Sanskrit language. Later she relinquished everything to Rajdhar and went to pilgrimage during last part of her life. Resident Leek wrote a letter to the Governor General Warren Hastings informing that Rajdhar was the choice of both the queen and the king to be the future king of their kingdom. (Mr. Leek's letter to Honourable Governor General, Warren Hasting, dated 5th July, 1783).

Queen Kamala Devi

Of course this custom of 'Sati' had been prevalent in the Royal Dynasties, as the Rajmala, the chronicle history of the Royal families recorded the events within the royal families. It is not known how much this custom was prevalent among other common tribal people of different communities.Rajmala recorded the 'Sati' of Kamala Devi in the 16th Century. The first two decades of the 18th

Century also recorded many sati queens in Ahom Rajdoot Ratnakandali and Arjun Das's description. In 1829, Lord William Bentick declared sati custom as illegal in India. But in Tripura it was continued for many more years and specially in Birchandra Manikya's time many proofs were found in Government letters that it was practiced particularly in Jamatia community. In 1888, the British Government Commissinor of Chittagang ordered the Assistant political agent Umakanta Das to investigate the matter. The Royal establishment admitted that the custom was not forcefully proclaimed but the tribal widows willingly embraced it. So there would be no need to bring out any official legal order. But the British Commissioner D. R Layal was not satisfied at this and pressurized the Tripura King Birchandra who later on was compelled to ban it in Tripura in 1889.

Queen Birangana

Even in the royal families of Tripura, Women were neither given any official power nor equal freedom though some queens were extremely potential and capable of facing any challenge. The Queen Birangana Tripura Sunadari who was also called as mahadevi was an extremely courageous and strong minded lady. She was the queen of 140th King of Tripura's Royal family Kirtidhan. In 1240, when the Muslim King of Guar invaded Tripura, the King Kirtidhan after getting scared of huge number of sultan's soldiers wanted to compromise. But the Queen Birangana encouraged her sons and ministers to take control of the war and accordingly she herself sat on elephant's shoulder and appeared on the war field. Under her able guidance the Tripura' soldiers could defeat the Sultan. From Pratima Roys's Birangana Tripura-a beautiful Bengali poem composed on this valorous act of the queen, we get an account of it.

The Guar soldiers have come like inferno, Your king acted like a jackal of den; But in the war ground, I myself will go, Let all come with me who are valorous men.

(Translated into English by the authoress herself)

Queen Gunabati

Gunabati was another kind-hearted queen who had great influence on her husband, the King Govinda Manikya. The nobel laureate Rabindra Nath Tagore wrote the novel 'Rajarshi' and the drama 'Bisarjan' on this king and the queen. From her name itself, it is quite evident that she had many qualities. She was extremely interested in village development. She dug a big pond which is reputed as 'Gunasagar'. According to the name of the queen, a village was named 'Guanbati' in Trishna Parganas. In 1668, she had built a Bishnu Temple at Udaipur. She was compassionate and kind hearted and showed benevolence by forgiving the Reang rebels, the story of which has been finely recorded in Surendra Dev Barman book's Tripurar Adhibasi- Jiban O Sanskiti'.

Queen Dwitiya Devi

Dwitiya Devi was another royal lady full of stamina and strength. She was the daughter of Jagannath Thakur, the younger brother of king Govinda Manikya, who dug a big pond in lower part of the Lalmai Hill (Dist. Of Comilla) in Meherkul Parganas. She also built two temples at the summit of Lalmai Hill. In one temple she set up the idol of Devi Chandika and accordingly the hill was named Chandimura later on. (Tripura Itihas Page- 78, J. Gon Choudhury).

Queen Prabhabati

Another very noteworthy royal lady was the Queen Pravabati Devi. Salil Krishna Debbarma in his article "Raj Amaley Chitrakala- Smriti Bismriti" described with beautiful language her expertise in painting. Pravabati Devi was the queen of Birendra Kishore and she was an extremely pious lady. She was encouraged by her husband, who knowing the potentiality and creativity of the queen inspired her, to take painting seriously.

The Princess

Kamala Prava Devi

She was another extremely talented royal artist who started her painting career at an early age. She painted mostly in water colour the different natural scene with articulate touch of her brush. All the natural scenes are as lively as nature herself. In her own classic style, she used colours with imaginative strokes. Though all her paintings bear the mark of art for art's sake emotional effect, yet her own distinct mark is quite evident that was unaffected by her predecessors.

Queen Tulsibati

Coming to the modern time the names of three royal ladies can be mentioned who as women are much forward than their male counterparts. And among them, the queen Tulsibati was the legendary women for first spreading the light of education in the lives of girls of Tripura. Tulsibati was born in the first part of 1860 in a poor peasant family at Nalgoria village of Ranir bazar at Agartala. Her original name was Angus Laime. According to some people, at the age of six, she was brought to the Royal family as the queen of Radha Kishore Manikya. It is not known authentically whether Tulsibati was literate but some of her own composed songs do bear the proof that if she was not literate it would not be possible to create such beautiful poems. One such poem on Radha and Shyam in colour spring is superbly well-knit by the Queen Tulsibati. The original piece of song in its native

(Bengali) form composed by the queen Tulsibati is given below.

"Gheri Gheri Sakhi sabe pulake matilo Jabe,

Abir kum kum Kasturi diteche Shyamer Ange,

Lal Lal Halo tanu, akulita raikanu,

Chura Kundal hele baje mohan basire!

Heri aparup rai kanu rup

Tulsibati Jeno rangapad herere."

Surrounded by friends, Radha was full of glee and gay

Scattering colours, vermilion and musk on Shyam in spray

Every one with Shyam and Radha enraptured in burgandy red

Bewildering tune of Shyam's flute sounds enchanting shed.

Beholding the spell of Radha and Shyam's Heavenly look

As humble bow on Lord's redfeet Tulsibati took.

(Translated by the authoress into English from Bengali)

But the most astonishing fact is her consciousness for girls and her awareness for their education though herself was illiterate (if we believe so) yet the whole women society of Tripura was in great debt to Tulsibati who understood it very clearly by her heart that without education and literacy, women could never stand on their own feet. And instead of demanding ornaments,clothes, and other decorative pieces which were common womanly desires she aspired for girls' education and accordingly wanted one girls' school within the imperial palace. That day it was a dream and today it is a golden history in the life of Tripura's women. In 1894 on 9th April, the school started it's journey with the name–'Agartala Balika Vidyalaya'. At first only girls of Royal families came to study there but gradually girls from far and near started joining here. The School was funded by the queen's personal treasury. No tuition fees were taken from the girls and prizes or rewards were given also in a new pattern. Instead of giving certificates or books, she gave away daily-use-materials like brass pot, plate, bowl or box etc. This was to encourage the poor illiterate parents who in lure of getting useful household things send their girls to school. Her germination of that infant school for girls becomes a large and huge institution named M.T.B. Girls' H.S. School where more than 3500 girls get the rare opportunity to study yearly. Within these hundred eleven years this prestigious institution has been able to produce many general and tribal women personalities who have taken the responsibilities all over India in different fields by showing their outstanding performances.

Tulsibati's benevolence does not stop here. She also did many other noble social works for women. In 1905, she,from her own treasure opened a female ward in Victoria Memorial Hospital, with ten beds to treat the women patients only and today this hospital has become Indira Gandhi Memorial Hospital with more than two hundred beds for children and women.

To remove the disadvantages of marketing for common people of remote areas who face great difficulty in shopping in village weekly 'hat', she arranged a market which is today named as Ranir Bazar. In 1908, she died of cancer. In creating the landmark,development for women education to give them proper dignity, strength and freedom, Maharani Tulsibati will be remembered for ever in the history of Women' Education in Tripura.

Anangamohini Devi

In the Royal family, the most noteworthy poetess was Ananga Mohini Devi who was the daughter of king Birchandra. She has in her credit three books of poems namely 'Kanika', 'Sokagatha' and 'Priti'. All these anthology books bear the mark of a very matured artist. Though it is not exactly recorded how far she was formally educated but it is a fact that her potentiality could have brought more colour if she got proper educational surrounding, training, encouragements and recognition. Her excellent originality reflected in the poems of Kanika that captivated even Rabindranath who praised her poetic genius highly.

Queen Kanchan Prabha

In 1947, on 17th May, the king Bir Bikram Kishore Manikya died at the age of only 39. At that time, his minor son, Kirit Bikram Kishore Manikya, though by inheritance entitled to everything yet for his minor age, his mother, the Queen Kanchan Prabha Devi took the charge as the regent on the advice of the Indian Government and under her guidance, formed the Council of Regency (17th May, 1947).

Queen Kanchanprabha Devi, after formation of the Council of Regency (17th May, 1947) became the independent president of it on 1948,12th January. Under her able guidance, when Pakisthan tried to invade Tripura on 3rd November, 1947, she made that attempt unsuccessful with the help of Indian Government through Assam State. In 1949, 9th September she signed the first historical agreement on behalf of her minor son for the inclusion of Tripura to Indian Union as one of the 'C' category States of India.

The queen has also gifted Tripura, her late husband's golden dream, a three year degree college at Agartala's College Tilla for which the king much before his death had already acquired a big plot of land on the Eastern side of Agartala town. After the king's death, Kanchanprava Devi contributed one lakh rupee from her Chakla Roshanabad fund to memorise the king's name and accordingly she christened the college after the king's name. This college named Maharaja Bir Bikram College is the pioneer institution in imparting the three year degree course, established in 1947 by the benevolence of the Regent Queen Kanchanprava Devi. Thus step by step advancement of education in Tripura has been done by the so called female brain, who themselves were not so educated but felt the urge and necessity of education and it is their contribution that helps to lit thousands of lights in almost all houses of Tripura.

Almost more than fifty years back, the Queen Kanchanprava Devi effectively exercised her political and official powers for the beneficial works of the state. Particularly at a period when the old kingdom of Tripura's Royal Dynasty was in turmoil and had given birth to a free state of Indian Territory, it was her able authority with strong personality as a widow Royal lady who did not allow Tripura to get into mess but put the foundation stone of democracy of modern Tripura. A proclamation regarding the administrative ruling of Tripura is recorded here to prove the above mentioned points.

CAMP SHILLONG

The 5th Calcutta, 1357 T. E

Proclamation of Her Highness the Regent Maharani Mahadevi

1. On the 18th December last in a statement issued to the press from Calcatta. I signified my intention to call, on my return to Agartala, a meeting of the Council of Regency with a view to preparing a declaration for the introduction of popular reforms in Tripura State.

On the 12th January, 1948, one day after my return to the State Capital on that occasion, the Council of Regency was, on the advice of the Government of India, dissolved. A new Chief Minister for the state had meanwhile been appointed on the recommendation of the Government of India and had just taken over the charge. In these circumstances some delay in issuing the promised further declaration much as I regret it was unavoidable.

2. In my statement of the 18th December I said that Tripura would have a fully democratic constitution. Such a constitution can be framed. I am now persuaded, not by any appointed body but by a body which is itself constituted on a properly democratic basis. It is my desire that, as early as conditions permit, steps will be taken to set up a constitution making body representative of all sections of the people which will be entrusted into the task of making such recommendations and tendering such advice to the Ruling power in regard to alteration or modification of, addition to and deletion from the present Government of Tripura Act (Act I of 1351 T.E.) as may appear desirable and necessary to this body.

3. The immediate task, however, is the maintenance of the stability of the State which has assumed a special significance and urgency in the context of the achievement of independence by India and her unfortunate partition in the process. A strong well organized internal security force has to be build up the finance of the State have to be rehabilitated, a scheme of road construction to provide internal communications as well as direct link with the Indian Union has to be put into effect, supplies of essential commodities of which there is an acute shortage have to be made available to the people, and the machinery of the government has to be general, tightened up. All

energies, for the present must be directed to the above ends.

4. Pending formation of the construction making body and the appointment of Ministers enjoying the confidence of that body I have decided, in exercises of the vested in me as the sole Regent by section 61 of the Government of Tripura Act (Act I 1351 T.E.) to keep in abeyance those provisions in Part III of the Act which relate to the constitution, appointment, powers, duties etc. of the Mantri Parisad or Council of Ministers and to dissolve the present Council of Ministers forthwith. It is my desire that the Government shall, for the present be carried on by the Chief Minister, who will hereafter be designed as the Dewan of Tripura State, with the assistance of one Adviser and two or three secretaries. In making this decision, I believe I am only giving effect to the wishes of my people.It has been long recognized that the present Council of Ministers could not be allowed to function indefinitely after the resignation in circumstances well known to my people, of the previous Chief Minister on whose recommendations the Council had been formed. The delay in making this necessary change is explained solely by the fact that the new Chief Minister had to be allowed sometime to pick up the threads before he could be called upon to assume full responsibility for the State Administration.
5. My attention has been drawn to certain reports published in the Calcutta Press and elsewhere about Tripura State being merged into Assam. None of these emanated from any authoritative source and there is absolutely no truth in them. I would ask my people not to be misled by such reports.
6. Lastly, let me remind my people again that this State is now passing through a period of extraordinary crisis

unprecedented in its long history. It is a challenge which the entire people of this state must take up as one body. It can be met only by unremitting hard work and undergoing sacrifice from all sections of the people, richer poor high or low. The future of the state which I am confident, will be even more glorious than its past rests with the people, with the introduction of responsible Government they will play a vital part in shaping it. It is my prayerful wish that their activities may, mean while be directed to constructive channels unimpeded by harmful difference or needless agitation so that by their united effort Tripura state, while retaining its own identity may in not very distinct future, contribute materially to strength and welfare of the Indian Union, as a whole.

Kanchan Prabha Devi
Regent Maharani

It has given much pleasure to learn that a Committee to raise funds for the Gandhi National Memorial Fund has been set up under the auspices of the Tripura State Congress with the approval of the Central, Indian Committee. The noble ideals of the other of the Nation and his sacred memory will, I am sure, bring together all sections of the people to contribute their mite towards the noble cause for which the fund is being raised and the schemes of which are already well known I wish the Committee all success.

K.P. Devi
Maharani Regent of Tripura

Source: Tripura Gazette Sankalan 1903- 1949 compiled and edited by Suprasanna Banerjee.

Maharani Bivu Devi

And lastly we may mention one important queen's name of modern Tripura, and that is Maharani Bivu Devi who is much advanced and qualified than her predecessors. In 1972 on 21st January, Tripura got full dignity and honour of a complete state of India Union and a new lease of life has started both historically and economically also. This new journey also touched the inner breeze of four walls of the Royal palaces. Maharani Bivu Devi, the wife of his Highness Kirit Bikram Manikya actually franchise her power as a woman. In 1988 she won the Assembly election from Matabari constituency and she was elected as a Congress M. P. in 1989 on S.T. seat. She was also elected as a cabinet minister for Revenue Department in 1988.

Thus with the whole world and specially with the rest of India, Tripura, the most economically backward tiny state is also not lagging far behind in women education and the germination of this female education had started, though extremely scanty in number more than hundred years before. It is really remarkable to think that in Tripura,before the girls' school established by Maharani Tulsibati, 'there were four girls' schools in 1880-81.The total number of girl students was 64.Of course all these students were of Manipuri Community because the kings of Tripura had mostly Manipuri queens and that was why Manipuri girls outnumbered others in getting the education. In 1882-83 the number of girls' school increased to six but in 1883-84 the number of these girls' school again decreased into two and in 1890-91 all the schools were closed. So it is clear that education for women was at that time in a transition period. Before that in 1874-75, there were only two schools, one at Agartala (1872) and the other at Kailasahar (1872) for a population of nearly 75,000. And these two schools had only 108 pupils on the rolls. In 1879,the number of schools and pupils had been on steady rise to 25 and 700 respectively, of 700 pupils, 57 were girls (3 belonging to Tripuri and 54 to Manipuri

Community). As the parents of that time did not prefer the co-educational establishments, the study of girls ended upto class-VIII. After M. T. B. the second girls' school was established in 1954 in Kailasahar and the third one in 1957 at Dharmanagar. The ST and SC students get free education with free school dress to spread the consciousness of education among them. Not only this, to make education popular among the girls, in 1958, the National Committee on Women education under the leadership of Smt. Durgamukh Deshmukh was formed and in Tripura also, the state committee of women education was established in 1964. To spread education among the tribal girls, many girls hostels, were built and in the first phase came Agartala M.T.B. Girls' Hostel, and Kailasahar and Belonia also got these girls Hostels. The next year in 1965 the first Women's College at Agartala with hostel facilities was opened for all communities. The ground was prepared and the seed was in, its germinated form. The Royal tribal women, though high in their status and empowerment did not enjoy the same facilities of freedom what the general and common women are getting today in education or social or economical or legal or mental or religious status. Yet the noteworthy point is that though these Royal women were denied all these modern and civilized facilities, there was no dearth of their courage, strength and stamina to usher in the awareness of good quality in lives for women which if they were given the opportunity and chance, they could have proved themselves much better than now as their dedication was pure to give sure results.

3
Position of Common Tribal Women in Tripura

The average girl children are never considered as asset in Indian society till today. In patriarchal society, girls are always treated in a neglected way under the dominance of man. Manu's adverse comment against women shows how undignified and servile was the position of women in both family and in society also. "Grant me a son and a girl elsewhere" was the prayer found in *Arthaveda*. The newly married bride and every woman were offered only one blessing - 'May you be the mother of hundred sons'. Even today, the modern bride is blessed with a son, because of modern science hundred sons have been reduced into one but the sex is same - a son and not a daughter which clearly shows the step motherly attitude towards the daughters.

Barring the developed countries of the world, almost all other countries developing and underdeveloped bear the same picture of an unbalanced gender based population where, females in every hundred males are much less in number. The different population charts of India on sex ratio and that of Tripura will prove this point.

In Table 2, the growth rate of population in Tripura shows a steady increase from the last part of the 19th Century to the middle part of the 20th Century and then up to 1991-2001, the average growth comes more or less into a fixed position.

In the Census Report of India 2001, the comparison of Tripura on population distribution, sex ratio and literacy rate with Indian States and Union Territories is shown.

Table 3, Tripura's four district's study of Sex ratio, population and growth rate and density are brought and it is found that West Tripura surpassed all other three districts on every level.

Table 4 will show the Sex ratio in detail in four districts of Tripura which indicates not much satisfactory female births till 2001.

Statement I show the rank of sex ratio in Tripura's four districts in which South Tripura stands first though the difference of female birth in four districts is quite negligible.

Table 5 will show the selected four tribe's population and the Tripuri is the highest in numbers.

Table 6 depicts the tribewise distribution of total tribal female population where also the Tripuri female population is highest.

Table 7 will show the growth of literacy among the S.T. and general in Tripura.

Table 8, The Districtwise Tribal Population of 1981, 1991 and 2001 Census is given.

Table 9 will show the S.T. Population of 1991 Census, Percentage of S.T.

Population by Male and Female literacy in Tripura (1991 Census) is shown in Table. 10.

In Table. 11 Literacy of S.T. Population according to 1991 census is given.

Table 1

Census of India 2001: Provisional Population totals Figures at a glance for India, States and Union Territories, Population, Sex-ratio, Population Density and Literacy

State/ UT Code	India/ State/ Union Territories	Population 2001			Sex-ratio (no. of female per 1000 men)		Population Density		Literacy Rate		
		Persons	Males	Females	1991	2001	1991	2001	Persons	Males	Females
1	2	3	4	5	6	7	8	9	10	11	12
	India 1, 2, 3	1027015247	531277078	495736169	972	933	267	324	65.38	75.85	54.16
1.	Jammu & Kashmir	10069917	5300574	476343	896	900	77	99	54.46	65.75	41.82
2.	Himachal Pradesh	6077248	3085256	4769343	976	970	93	109	77.13	86.02	68.08
3.	Punjab	24289296	12963362	11325934	882	874	403	482	69.95	75.63	63.55
4.	Chandigarh	900914	508224	392690	790	773	5632	7903	81.76	85.65	76.65
5.	Uttaranchal	8479562	4316401	4163161	936	964	133	169	72.28	84.01	60.26
6.	Harayana	21082989	11327658	9755331	865	861	372	477	68.59	79.25	56.31
7.	Delhi	13782976	7570890	6212086	827	821	6352	9294	81.82	87.37	75.00
8.	Rajasthan	56473122	29381657	27091465	910	922	129	165	61.03	76.46	44.34
9.	U.P.	166052859	87466301	78586558	876	898	548	689	57.36	70.23	42.98

(Contd...)

(Contd...)

State/ UT Code	India/ State/ Union Territories	Population 2001			Sex-ratio (no. of female per 1000 men)		Population Density		Literacy Rate		
		Persons	Males	Females	1991	2001	1991	2001	Persons	Males	Females
1	2	3	4	5	6	7	8	9	10	11	12
10.	Bihar	82878796	43153964	39724832	907	921	685	880	47.53	60.32	35.37
11.	Sikkim	540493	288217	252276	878	876	57	76	69.68	76.73	61.46
12.	Arunachal Pradesh	1091117	573951	517166	859	901	10	13	54.74	64.74	44.24
13.	Nagaland	1988636	1041686	946950	886	909	73	120	67.11	71.77	61.92
14.	Manipur	2388634	1207338	1181296	958	978	82	107	68.87	77.87	59.70
15.	Mizoram	891058	459783	431275	951	938	33	42	88.49	90.69	86.13
16.	Tripura	3191168	1636138	1555030	945	950	263	304	73.66	81.47	65.41
17.	Meghalaya	2306069	116780	1138229	955	979	79	103	63.31	63.14	60.41
18.	Assam	26638407	13787799	12850608	923	932	286	340	64.28	71.93	56.03
19.	W.B.	80221171	41487694	38733477	917	934	767	904	69.22	77.58	60.22
20.	Jharkhand	28909428	13861277	13046151	922	941	274	338	54.13	67.94	39.28

(Contd...)

(Contd...)

State/ UT Code	India/ State/ Union Territories	Population 2001			Sex-ratio (no. of female per 1000 men)		Population Density		Literacy Rate		
		Persons	Males	Females	1991	2001	1991	2001	Persons	Males	Females
1	2	3	4	5	6	7	8	9	10	11	12
21.	Orissa	36706920	18612340	18094580	971	972	203	236	63.61	75.91	50.97
22.	Chattisgarh	207956	10452426	10343530	985	990	130	154	65.18	77.86	52.40
23.	M.P.	60385118	31456873	28928245	912	920	158	196	64.11	76.80	50.28
24.	Gujrat	50596992	26344053	24252939	934	921	211	258	69.97	80.50	58.60
25.	Daman & Diu	158059	92478	65581	969	739	907	1411	81.09	88.40	70.37
26.	Dadra & Nagar Havell	220451	1217321	98720	952	811	282	449	60.03	73.32	42.99
27.	Maharashtra	96752247	50334270	46417977	934	922	257	314	77.27	86.27	67.51
28.	Andhra Pradesh	75727541	38286811	37440730	972	978	242	275	61.11	70.85	51.12
29.	Karnataka	52733958	26856343	25877615	960	964	235	275	67.04	76.29	57.45
30.	Goa	1343996	685617	658381	967	960	316	363	82.32	88.88	75.51

(Contd...)

(Contd...)

State/ UT Code	India/ State/ Union Territories	Population 2001			Sex-ratio (no. of female per 1000 men)		Population Density		Literacy Rate		
		Persons	Males	Females	1991	2001	1991	2001	Persons	Males	Females
1	2	3	4	5	6	7	8	9	10	11	12
31.	Lakshadweep	60595	31118	29477	943	947	1616	1894	87.52	93.15	81.56
32.	Kerala	31838619	15468664	16369955	1036	1058	749	819	90.92	94.20	87.86
33.	Tamil Nadu	62110839	31268654	30842185	974	986	429	478	73.47	82.33	64.55
34.	Pondicherry	973829	486805	487124	979	1001	1683	2029	81.49	88.89	74.13
35.	Andaman & Nicobar	356265	192985	163280	818	846	34	43	81.18	86.07	75.29

Table 2
Tripura's Demographic Change: 1874-1991, 2001

Year	*Total Population*	*Percentage Variation*	*Tribal Population*	*Percentage of Tribal to Total Population*
1874-75	74242	—	47523	64
1881	95635	28.82	49915	52.19
1891	137575	43.85	70292	51.09
1901	173325	25.99	91697	52.89
1911	229613	32.48	111303	48.47
1921	304347	32.59	171610	56.37
1931	382450	25.63	203327	52.00
1941	513010	34.14	256991	50.09
1951	639028	24.56	237953	37.23
1961	1142005	78.71	360070	31.50
1971	1556342	36.28	450544	28.95
1981	2053058	31.92	583920	28.44
1991	2744827	34.30	853345	30.95
2001	3191168	16.26	993426	31.05

Source: W.W. Hunter, p. 484.
S. Deb Barma, Census Bibarani 1931; Census of India, Series 1, paper 2 of 1992, Final Population Total; A Brief Analysis of Primary Census Abstract, pp. 98-100.

Table 3
Population Distribution, Percentage Decadal Growth Rate, Sex-Ratio and Population Density for States and Districts

Sl. No.	*State/District*	*Population 2001*			*Percentage decadal Growth rate*		*Sex-ratio (No. of females per 1000 males)*		*Population density per sq. km.*	
		Persons	*Male*	*Females*	*1981-91*	*1991-01*	*1991*	*2001*	*1991*	*2001*
1	2	3	4	5	6	7	8	9	10	11
	TRIPURA	3191168	1636138	1535030	34.30	15.7	945	950	263	304
1.	West Tripura District	1530531	783825	746706	32.63	18.2	944	953	427	505
2.	South Tripura District	762565	391109	37386	40.30	26.0	951	949	229	243
3.	Dhalai District	307417	158480	148937	33.69	10.7	931	940	125	139
4.	North Tripura District	590655	302654	288001	30.86	26.4	943	952	222	281

Table 4

Sex Ratio Since 1901 for State and District

Sl. No.	*State / District*	*1901*	*1911*	*1921*	*1931*	*1941*	*1951*	*1961*	*1971*	*1981*	*1991*	*2001*
1	2	3	4	5	6	7	8	9	10	11	12	13
	TRIPURA	874	885	885	886	904	932	943	943	946	945	950
1.	West Tripura District	877	891	893	891	881	908	937	946	954	944	953
2.	South Tripura District	874	884	881	873	878	909	937	946	946	951	949
3.	Dhalai District	877	886	888	896	911	908	932	932	938	931	940
4.	North Tripura District	856	866	868	879	895	886	909	935	931	943	952

Table 5
Selected Tribewise Population

Sl. No.	*Tribe*	*1961*	*1971*	*1981*	*1991*	*2001*
1.	Tripuri	189799	250545	330872	461531	543848
2.	Riang	56597	64722	84004	111606	165103
3.	Jamatia	24359	34192	44501	60824	74949
4.	Chakma	22386	28622	34797	96096	64293

Source: Census Report (1991 and 2001.)

Table 6
Tribewise Composition of Tribal Female Population to Total Female Population in 1961, 1971, 1981, and 2001 Tripura

	1961	*1971*	*1981*	*1991*	*2001*
Total Tribal	100.00	100.00	100.00	100.00	100.00
Tripuri	52.80	55.64	56.77	54.08	54.80
Riang	15.70	14.20	14.33	13.04	16.55
Jamatia	6.32	7.68	7.73	7.23	7.64
Chakma	6.11	6.19	5.90	11.26	6.40
Halam	4.48	4.19	5.00	4.30	4.78
Mag	2.89	2.92	3.08	3.66	3.06
Remaining thirteen	11.70	9.18	7.19	—	—

Source: Census of India 1961, Vol. XXVI, Tripura Part III and V-A; Census of India 1971, Series 20 Tripura, Part IIC(i) and Part V-A; Census of India 1981; Series 21 Tripura, Part-IX; State/District Primary Census Abstract of 1991 (provisional), Tripura.

Table 7
Growth of Literacy among the Tribals

Year	*Literacy among Scheduled Tribes*	*General Literacy in the State*
1961	10.01	20.24
1971	15.03	30.39
1981	23.07	42.12
1991	32.25	60.39
2001	56.48	73.66

Note: In 1991 Census all children below age 7 have been treated as illiterate. In 1961, 1971, 1981 and 2001 Censuses all the children below 5 years weretreated as illiterates.

Source: Census reports 1961, 1971, 1981, 1991 and 2001 (provisional).

Table 8
Tribal Population by Tribes and District (1981-2001 Census)
1981

	Total Tripura				West Tripura			North Tripura			South Tripura		
Name of Scheduled tribes	*Persons*	*% of total population*	*Males*	*Females*	*Persons*	*Males*	*Females*	*Persons*	*Males*	*Females*	*Persons*	*Males*	*Females*
1	2	3	4	5	6	7	8	9	10	11	12	13	14
All Scheduled Tribes	583920	28.44	297612	286308	244146	123398	120748	147884	76090	71794	191890	98124	93766
1. Bhil	838	0.04	450	388	378	204	174	43	23	20	417	223	194
2. Bhutia	22	0.00	14	8	6	3	3	7	3	4	9	8	1
3. Chaimal	18	0.00	11	7	1	—	1	15	9	6	2	2	—
4. Chakma	34799	1.69	17966	16833	81	41	40	20897	10855	10042	13821	7070	9751
5. Garoo	7297	0.36	3632	3665	1370	637	733	2930	1491	1439	2997	1504	1493
6. Halam	28969	1.41	14666	14303	7968	3960	4008	9266	4720	4546	11735	5986	5749
7. Jamatia	44501	2.17	22368	22133	8282	4165	4117	263	140	123	35956	18063	17893

(Contd...)

(Contd...)

1981

Name of Scheduled tribes	Total Tripura				West Tripura			North Tripura			South Tripura		
	Persons	% of total population	Males	Females	Persons	Males	Females	Persons	Males	Females	Persons	Males	Females
1	2	3	4	5	6	7	8	9	10	11	12	13	14
8. Khasia	457	0.02	235	222	18	10	8	427	222	205	12	3	9
9. Kuki (Int.) Sub-Tribes*	5501	0.87	3831	2970	664	354	310	4024	2055	1969	813	422	391
10. Lepcha	106	0.01	49	57	85	37	48	9	6	3	12	6	6
11. Lushai	3734	0.18	1936	1798	119	71	48	3555	1831	1724	60	34	26
12. Naga	18231	0.89	9389	8842	276	137	139	1688	876	812	16267	8376	7891
13. Munda Kaur	7993	0.39	4190	3803	5236	2737	2499	2159	1137	1022	598	316	282
14. Noatia	7181	0.35	3695	3486	2156	1112	1044	2093	1087	1006	2932	1496	143

(Contd...)

(Cont...)

1981

Name of Scheduled tribes	Total Tripura				West Tripura			North Tripura			South Tripura		
	Persons	% of total population	Males	Females	Persons	Males	Females	Persons	Males	Females	Persons	Males	Females
1	2	3	4	5	6	7	8	9	10	11	12	13	14
15. Orang	5217	0.25	2670	2547	2342	1215	1127	2591	1296	1295	283	159	124
16. Riang	84005	4.09	42973	41032	2413	1254	1159	47235	24233	23002	34357	17486	16871
17. Santal	2725	0.13	1428	1297	1745	919	826	399	205	194	581	304	277
18. Tripuri, Tripura, Tippera	330872	16.12	168334	162538	210923	106476	104447	50263	25884	24379	69686	35974	33712
19. Uchai	1306	0.06	670	636	10	7	3	1	1	—	1295	662	633

(Contd...)

(Contd...)

1991

Name of Scheduled tribes	Total Tripura				West Tripura				North Tripura				South Tripura			
	Persons	% of total population	Males	Females	Persons	Perce-ntage	Males	Females	Persons	Perce-ntage	Males	Females	Persons	Perce-ntage	Males	Females
1	2	3	4	5	6	7	8	9	10	11	12	13	14	15	16	17
All Scheduled Tribes	853345	30.94	434225	419120	325845	42.53	165554	160291	197975	28.39	101596	96379	329525	25.46	167075	162450
1. Bhil	1754	0.06	921	833	698	0.09	379	319	118	0.01	58	60	938	0.07	484	454
2. Bhutia	47	0.00	27	20	5	0.00	4	1	18	0.00	13	5	24	0.00	10	14
3. Chaimal	26	0.00	18	8	9	0.00	9	0	8	0.00	4	4	9	0.00	5	4
4. Chakma	96096	3.48	48886	47210	273	0.03	162	111	32428	4.65	16776	15652	63395	4.89	31948	31447
5. Garoo	9360	0.33	4734	4626	1461	0.19	740	721	3914	0.56	1994	1920	3985	0.30	2000	1985
6. Halam	36499	0.01	18462	18037	9522	1.24	4774	4748	11786	1.69	5988	5798	15191	1.17	7700	7491
7. Jamatia	60824	2.20	30517	30307	9500	1.24	4811	4689	518	0.07	280	238	50806	0.03	25426	25380

(Contd...)

(Contd...)

1991

Name of Scheduled tribes	Total Tripura Persons	% of total population	Males	Females	West Tripura Persons	Perce-ntage	Males	Females	North Tripura Persons	Perce-ntage	Males	Females	South Tripura Persons	Perce-ntage	Males	Females
1	2	3	4	5	6	7	8	9	10	11	12	13	14	15	16	17
8. Khasia	358	0.01	185	173	85	0.01	45	40	238	0.03	122	116	35	0.00	18	17
9. Kuki (Int.) Sub-Tribes*	10628	0.38	5451	5177	2321	0.30	1176	1145	6226	0.89	3213	3013	2081	0.16	1062	1019
10. Lepcha	111	0.00	52	59	42	0.00	23	19	46	0.00	21	25	23	0.00	8	15
11. Lushai	4910	0.17	2522	2388	194	0.02	107	87	4555	0.65	2344	2211	161	0.01	71	90
12. Mag	31612	1.14	16242	15370	409	0.05	226	183	3942	0.56	2063	1879	27261	2.10	13953	13308
13. Munda Kaur	11547	0.41	5964	5583	6959	0.90	3588	3371	3023	0.43	1572	1451	1565	0.12	804	761
14. Noatia	4158	0.15	2148	2010	1885	0.24	980	905	62	0.00	38	24	2211	0.17	1130	1081

(Contd...)

(Contd...)

1991

Name of Scheduled tribes	Total Tripura: Persons	Total Tripura: % of total population	Total Tripura: Males	Total Tripura: Females	West Tripura: Persons	West Tripura: Percentage	West Tripura: Males	West Tripura: Females	North Tripura: Persons	North Tripura: Percentage	North Tripura: Males	North Tripura: Females	South Tripura: Persons	South Tripura: Percentage	South Tripura: Males	South Tripura: Females
1	2	3	4	5	6	7	8	9	10	11	12	13	14	15	16	17
15. Orang	6751	0.24	3430	3321	3049	0.39	1600	1449	3483	0.49	1717	1766	219	0.01	113	106
16. Riang	111606	4.04	56944	54662	3178	0.41	1654	1524	54589	7.82	27969	26620	53839	4.16	27321	26518
17. Santal	2736	0.09	1471	1265	2165	0.28	1152	1013	397	0.05	219	178	174	0.01	100	74
18. Tripuri, Tripura, Tippera	461531	16.73	234853	226678	283618	0.37	143905	139713	72085	10.33	36927	35158	105828	0.08	54021	51807
19. Uchai	1637	0.05	835	802	30	0.00	16	14	41	0.00	27	14	1566	0.12	792	774
20. Unclassified	1154	0.04	563	591	442	0.05	203	239	498	0.07	251	247	214	0.01	109	105

(Contd...)

(Contd...)

2001

	Total Tripura				West Tripura				North Tripura				South Tripura			
Name of Scheduled tribes	Persons	% of total population	Males	Females	Persons	Perce-ntage	Males	Females	Persons	Perce-ntage	Males	Females	Persons	Perce-ntage	Males	Females
1	2	3	4	5	6	7	8	9	10	11	12	13	14	15	16	17
All Scheduled Tribes	993426	31.13	504320	489106	387081	25.29	196094	190987	150500	25.48	77076	73424	289519	37.96	146051	143468
1. Bhil	2336	0.07	1210	1126	594	0.03	314	280	247	0.00	133	114	1490	0.19	761	729
2. Bhutia	29	0.00	17	12	15	0.00	7	8	9	0.00	7	2	5	0.00	3	2
3. Chaimal	226	0.00	115	111					93	0.01	55	38	50	0.00	24	26
4. Chakma	64293	2.01	32951	31342	398	0.02	212	186	23926	4.05	12349	11577	16027	2.10	8090	7937
5. Garoo	11180	0.35	5613	5567	1759	0.11	886	873	509	0.08	279	230	4826	0.63	2393	2433
6. Halam	47245	1.48	23861	2384	11287	0.73	5666	5621	1134	0.19	592	542	609	0.07	378	231
7. Jamatia	74949	2.34	37542	37407	12365	0.80	6400	5965	7393	0.01	3766	3627	19420	2.54	9792	9628

(Contd...)

(Contd...)

2001

		Total Tripura				West Tripura				North Tripura				South Tripura			
	Name of Scheduled tribes	Persons	% of total population	Males	Females	Persons	Percentage	Males	Females	Persons	Percentage	Males	Females	Persons	Percentage	Males	Females
	1	2	3	4	5	6	7	8	9	10	11	12	13	14	15	16	17
8.	Khasia	630	0.01	342	288	184	0.01	101	83	49	0.00	42	7	59918	7.85	29768	30150
9.	Kuki (Int.) Sub-Tribes*	11674	0.36	5894	5780	334587	21.86	169092	165495	295	0.04	159	136	–	–	–	–
10.	Lepcha	105	0.00	53	52	61	0.00	30	31	30	0.00	14	16	14	0.00	9	5
11.	Lushai	4777	0.14	2424	2553	62	0.00	42	20	2648	0.78	2346	2302	47	0.00	26	21
12.	Mag	30385	0.95	15393	14992	423	0.02	222	201	1487	0.25	757	730	24706	3.23	12510	12196
13.	Munda Kaur	12416	0.38	6367	6049	6907	0.45	3520	3387	2160	0.36	1139	1021	2125	0.27	1063	1062
14.	Noatia	6655	0.20	3401	3254	3472	0.22	1789	1683	8	0.00	5	3	2331	0.30	1183	1148

(Contd...)

(Contd...)

2001

Name of Scheduled tribes	Total Tripura Persons	% of total population	Males	Females	West Tripura Persons	Percentage	Males	Females	North Tripura Persons	Percentage	Males	Females	South Tripura Persons	Percentage	Males	Females
1	2	3	4	5	6	7	8	9	10	11	12	13	14	15	16	17
15. Orang	6223	0.19	3200	3023	2209	0.14	1166	1043	3696	0.62	1837	1859	122	0.01	77	45
16. Riang	165103	0.51	84155	80948	2975	0.19	1576	1399	80279	13.59	40991	39288	49698	6.51	25113	24585
17. Santal	2151	0.06	1189	962	1870	0.12	1021	849	206	0.03	121	85	13	0.00	11	2
18. Tripuri, Tripura, Tippera	543848	17.04	275784	268064	334587	0.21	169092	165495	18629	3.15	9567	9062	105333	13.81	53474	51859
19. Uchai	2103	0.00	1032	1071	53	0.00	32	21	24	0.00	13	11	2015	0.26	980	1035

1. Baite, 2. Belalhut, 3. Chhalya, 4. Fun, 5. Hajango, 6. Jangoei, 7. Khareng, 8. Khephog, 9. Kuntei, 10. Laifang, 11. Lentei, 12. Mizel, 13. Namtei, 14. Paitu, Paite, 15. Rangclan, 16. Rangkhole, 17. Thangulya.

Source: 1981 Cencus Publication series 21: Tripura (Part IX)

Note: All Schedule Tribe includes the figure of unclassified. 0.00–Negligible.

Dhalai District
2001

		Dhalai District			
	Name of Scheduled tribes	Persons	% of total population	Males	Females
	1	2	3	4	5
	All Scheduled Tribes	166326	54.10	85099	81227
1.	Bhil	5	0.00	2	3
2.	Bhutia	–	–	–	–
3.	Chaimal	80	0.02	34	46
4.	Chakma	23942	7.78	12300	11642
5.	Garoo	4086	1.32	2055	2031
6.	Generic Tribes etc.	483	0.15	261	222
7.	Halam	9145	2.97	4637	4508
8.	Jamatia	2617	0.85	1332	1285
9.	Khasia	151	0.04	82	69
10.	Lepcha	–	–	–	–
11.	Lushai	20	0.00	10	10

(Contd...)

(Contd...)

	Name of Scheduled tribes	Persons	% of total population	Males	Females
			Dhalai District		
	1	2	3	4	5
12.	Mag	3769	1.22	1904	1865
13.	Munda etc.	1224	0.39	645	579
14.	Noatia	844	0.27	424	420
15.	Orang	196	0.06	120	76
16.	Riang	32151	10.45	16475	15676
17.	Santal	62	0.02	36	26
18.	Tripura etc.	85629	0.27	9567	9062
19.	Uchai	11	0.00	7	4

Table 9
Scheduled Tribes Population According to Population Census 1991

District/Sub-division	Scheduled Tribes									Scheduled Tribes as percentage of Total Population
	Rural			Urban			Total			
	Persons	Males	Females	Persons	Males	Females	Persons	Males	Females	
1	2	3	4	5	6	7	8	9	10	11
1. West Tripura	314740	159804	154936	11105	5750	5355	325845	165554	160291	25.18
Sadar	186732	94754	91978	9720	4946	4774	196452	99700	96752	23.20
Khowai	108252	54951	53301	1308	755	553	109560	55706	53854	40.19
Sonamura	19756	10099	9657	77	49	28	19833	10148	9685	11.36
2. North Tripura	195883	100401	95482	2092	1195	897	197975	101596	96379	28.39
Dharmanagar	70265	36149	34116	358	234	124	70623	36383	34240	23.54

(Contd ...)

(Contd...)

District/Sub-division	Scheduled Tribes Rural			Scheduled Tribes Urban			Scheduled Tribes Total			Scheduled Tribes as percentage of Total Population
	Persons	Males	Females	Persons	Males	Females	Persons	Males	Females	
1	2	3	4	5	6	7	8	9	10	11
Kailashahar	83600	42697	40903	1601	870	731	85201	43567	41634	33.53
Kamalpur	42018	21555	20463	183	91	42	42151	216486	20505	29.43
3. South Tripura	328641	166536	162105	884	539	345	329525	167075	162450	43.02
Udaipur	51315	25712	25603	308	167	141	51623	45879	25744	24.62
Amarpur	112848	56834	56016	253	159	94	113101	56993	56108	71.64
Gandachhera	40227	20553	19674	—	—	—	40227	20553	19674	82.24
Belonia	61461	31375	30086	75	47	28	61536	31422	30114	26.67
Sabroom	62790	32062	30728	248	166	82	63038	32228	30810	53.05
Total Tripura	**839264**	**426741**	**412523**	**14081**	**7484**	**6597**	**853343**	**434225**	**419120**	**30.95**

Source: 1981 Census data (NIC).

Table 10

Percentage of Scheduled Tribe population by Male and Female Literacy in Tripura (1991-Census)

District/Sub-Division	*Literate population as percentage of total population (1991 Census)*		
	Male	*Female*	*Total*
1	2	3	4
West Tripura	66.00	38.56	52.53
Sadar	66.35	38.27	52.56
Khowai	68.50	42.65	55.80
Sonamura	48.39	17.71	33.56
North Tripura	50.95	25.59	38.65
Dharmanagar	56.92	29.50	43.98
Kanchanpur	51.90	26.17	39.44
Kailashahar	52.68	27.06	40.15
Longtharai	44.49	18.71	32.00
Kamalpur	56.33	32.71	44.84
South Tripura	41.15	17.39	29.47
Udaipur	54.05	29.25	41.68
Amarpur	39.57	16.46	28.12
Gandachhara	30.07	8.21	19.40
Belonia	43.74	18.71	31.56
Sabroom	38.27	13.72	26.35
Total Tripura	**52.88**	**27.34**	**40.37**

Note: Population aged 7 years and above.

Table 11

Area and Population Literacy of Scheduled Tribes Population According to Population (1991 Census)

District/ Sub-division	*Literate Population*									*Percentage of literates (Population aged 7 years and above)*
	Rural			**Urban**			**Total**			
	Persons	*Males*	*Females*	*Persons*	*Males*	*Females*	*Persons*	*Males*	*Females*	
1	2	3	4	5	6	7	8	9	10	11
West Tripura	127885	82716	45169	8652	4629	4023	136537	87345	49192	52.53
Sadar	74931	49051	25881	7768	4058	3710	82699	53108	29591	52.56
Khowai	47898	29898	18000	821	526	295	48711	30424	18295	55.80
Sonamura	5056	3768	1288	63	45	18	5119	3813	1306	33.56
North Tripura	59230	40214	19016	1250	831	419	60480	41045	19435	38.65
Dharmanagar	2719	1853	866	267	188	79	2986	2041	945	43.98
Kanchanpur	19518	13241	6277	—	—	—	19518	13241	6277	39.44
Kailashahar	7221	4859	2362	874	567	307	8095	5426	2669	40.15
Longtharai	14956	10706	4250	—	—	—	14956	10706	4250	32.00

(Contd...)

(Contd...)

District/ Sub-division	*Literate Population*									*Percentage of literates (Population aged 7 years and above)*
	Rural			**Urban**			**Total**			
	Persons	*Males*	*Females*	*Persons*	*Males*	*Females*	*Persons*	*Males*	*Females*	
1	*2*	*3*	*4*	*5*	*6*	*7*	*8*	*9*	*10*	*11*
Kamalpur	14816	9555	5261	109	76	33	14925	9631	5294	44.84
South Tripura	77523	50091	22432	716	454	262	78239	55545	22694	29.47
Udaipur	17019	11087	5932	254	135	119	17273	11222	6051	41.68
Amarpur	25960	18438	7522	192	130	62	26152	18568	7584	28.12
Gandacharra	6226	4940	1286	—	—	—	6226	4940	1286	19.40
Belonia	15161	10787	4374	55	37	18	15216	10824	4392	31.56
Sabroom	13156	9839	3318	215	152	63	13372	9991	3381	26.35
Total Tripura	**264638**	**178021**	**86617**	**10618**	**5914**	**4704**	**275256**	**183935**	**91321**	**40.37**

Note: 1991 Census data.

Table 12
School Drop Out Rates from Classes I-V
For the Year 1989-99 and 2000-2001. (in percentage)

Category	*1998-99*	*2000-2001*
Overall	53.11	50.60
S.C.	49.49	44.93
S.T.	66.58	63.59

Table 13
School Drop Out Rates from Classes I-VIII
For the Year 1998-99 and 2000-2001. (in percentage)

Category	*1998-99*	*2000-2001*
Overall	68.35	65.12
S.C.	67.16	62.00
S.T.	81.54	77.92

Table 14
School Drop Out Rates from Classes I-X
For the Year 1998-99 and 2000-2001. (in percentage)

Category	*1998-99*	*2000-2001*
Overall	80.17	76.95
S.C.	80.41	76.29
S.T.	88.14	86.72

Table 15
Districtwise S.T. Population
As per 1991 Census

Sl. No.	*Name of the District*	*Total Population*	*S.T. Population*	*Percentage of S.T. Population To Total District Population*
1	*2*	*3*	*4*	*5*
1.	West Tripura	1293861	325845	25.18
2.	North Tripura	467147	96463	20.65
3.	South Tripura	717100	289298	40.34
4.	Dhalai District	279097	141739	50.78
	Total	2757205	853345	30.94

Districtwise S.T. Population
As per 2001 Census

Sl. No.	*Name of the District*	*Total Population*	*S.T. Population*	*Percentage of S.T. Population To Total District Population*
1	*2*	*3*	*4*	*5*
1.	West Tripura	1530531	387081	25.29
2.	North Tripura	590655	150500	25.48
3.	South Tripura	762565	289519	37.96
4.	Dhalai District	307417	166326	54.10
	Total	3191168	993426	31.13

Table 16
Table Showing the Literacy Levels among the Scheduled Tribes

Year	*General Literacy*			*Literacy in Scheduled Tribes*		
	Male	*Female*	*Total*	*Male*	*Female*	*Total*
1	2	3	4	5	6	7
1961	29.61	10.19	20.24	17.37	2.31	10.01
1971	40.20	21.19	30.98	21.60	6.04	15.03
1981	51.17	32.00	42.12	33.46	12.27	23.07
1991	70.58	49.55	60.44	52.88	27.34	40.37
2001	81.47	65.41	73.66	N.A.	N.A.	56.48

The School Dropout rates from 1998 and onwards are shown in Table 12, 13, and 14 respectvel.

Districtwise S.T. Population as per 1991, 2001 census is shown in Table 15.

Table 16 shows the literacy level.

If we analyze the chart, Tripura's condition is much more better than rest of India both on the basis of female population and also in the rate of female literacy. We will now see the Tribal population and literacy particularly on female base. The 2001 census of S.T. are yet to be published and so we take up to 1991 census, and we analyze on that basis. See Table 2-7 and the statement 1A.

All these tables show that females are not only less developed in their literacy rate but also lower in birth rate. It is clear that female children is mostly unwanted and sometimes they are not allowed to take birth even. As the female birth is restricted, the same reason poses more restriction on their literacy rate.

In the tribal society though the birth of a girl child is not considered so much unwanted, or inauspicious or a liability as girls are needed for every household work from dawn to dusk, outside works like field work, water fetching, firewood collecting etc. and absence of dowry for girl's marriage are some of the important reasons which do not bring any headache to tribal parents. The excessive work load, malnutrition early marriage and repeated motherhood for tribal girls are there of course. The tribal people are not habituated to use scientific means to restrict their family. Yet the number of females are less in them which is really a matter of concern. One general analysis is that when people shift from one place to another for new settlement, the male members move first and leave behind their females. In search of daily livelihood also, men don't take their family along with them. This may be the reason of less number of females in counting by census.

So long, particularly before the accession of Tripura into Indian Union, no fruitful attempt so long has been taken to impart education among the hill people. The hill people were also rather indifferent and totally careless towards the development of the plain people with their gradual expansion of education. General feeling in those days was that education made their children defiant and alienated them from the society. And so education was perceived by these ignorant hill people as a sort of hedonism. They need the labour of their children either to attend to their homes, to look after the little brothers and sisters and to do all sorts of other household work while they attend to their jhums. It was also their idea that education tended to make their children baboos like plain people and made them adverse to the rough and tough work of the tribal society particularly the jhums.

So while the boys of these hill people are not allowed or sometimes they themselves are not willing to attend the school to taste fruit of literacy, it is unthinkable for girls to go for education. It is also for the fact that the tribals are economically independent in cultivating jhum, and their extremely simple life style make it enough for their daily bread. The little amount of cloth woven in their own loom suffices their need of want. Therefore, to go outside to do study does not arise for them. The life of the tribal women in the past was hard and arduous as they were totally enchained into household drudgeries. And naturally they were much underprivileged and under developed than men. As the division of labour in the family is gender based, a tribal woman who is generally married very early, has to do diversified works from dawn to dusk. She starts her day from sweeping, fetching water from far away, cleaning the house, cooking for family members, feeding the child, lulling it to sleep. Her next phase of work starts with bringing fire woods from nearby forest, then threshing the paddy seeds and stock them. Mostly she is to go paddy field to cultivate, to reap the crops. Back home she sits for spinning and then for evening cooking, serving, preparing beds and so on. Thus just like an untiring machine, a tribal woman changes her shifting duties from one phase to another of unpaid loads of huge works. In these ways, the tribal women in most of the time, do both the household work alongside a great deal of field work. In this long chain of work, there is no gap where a tribal woman can think for herself to acquire the luxury of education by spending few hours for it.

Besides, the lack of awareness for education among the tribal people, the extremely meagre presence and establishment of schools except few at Agartala are another bar for spreading of education among the tribal mass. The educational backwardness among the tribal communities is due to the differences in the provisions of educational facilities, socio-economic status of the parents, lack of motivation as a result of isolation, lack of communication and social distance.

So when non tribal women in general did not get much expected education, the education in tribal girls remained a far off thing at least in the 19th century and also the first half of the twentieth century. At that time, only some few girls belonging to the rich or the royal families and of the same level could be able to get to some extent a little education and that also from privately engaged teachers and tutors. During the British rule, acquisition of education became a privilege of the wealthy and upper middle class people and higher caste groups. Education became a status symbol and English, being the language of instruction and communication, the mass population was prevented from being educated. The first support for women education came from the missionaries who were in favour of educating women of remote and far flung areas as they used to work in these underdeveloped areas for charitable and religious ground. After the attempt of the missionaries, the British Government also undertook the task of spreading education to some extent. Yet the mass, particularly the rural population remained unaffected by this move.

This picture is not only true for Tripura but also for other neighbouring states like Bengal (also East Bengal which is now Bangladesh) and northeast states like Assam etc. Despite missionary or native ventures, the cause of female education in Bengal could not make steadily with the people during 1819-82. The Zenana Association (1883) through their peripatetic teachers put some 50,000 girls to instructions at home. This trend of female education was continued for next twenty years at many prominent places of East Bengal like Sylhet, Bikrampur, Faridpore, Bakhrganj, Mymensingh, Tipperah etc. under the able guidance of 'Abala Bandhava Dwaraknath'. The entrance level girls' schools namely Bethune School (1856), Victorica School (1886), Brahma Balika Vidhyala (1891), Sister Nivedita's Baghbazar Girls' School (1892) were all Calcutta based schools. During this same period, Dacca also had its female education programme underway in Eden Female School (1887-88).Despite this effort for throughout a century the result of women education was not very impressive and satisfactory within 1900-01, only 2.49 per cent of girls received education and within 1906-07, there were only 680 girls in H. S. Schools, 1776 in M.E. and 653 in M.V. Schools. In other words girls education had just started to germinate in Bengal. Let us come back to our Tripura's female education. In 1871, it was reported that a school known as Maharaja's school was established at Agartala, the state capital. The pupils all belonged to Raja's family excluding his sons who were given tuition privately in English. Some other influential men's sons also got the chance to attend this school while the hill people were totally left without any school or education and nothing had been done them.

By the end of 1872, another school was founded at Kailasahar with 8 to 9 students. In 1873-74 there were only 79 pupils in Maharaja school and all these pupils were male. In 1879, the number of schools and pupils had been on steady increase and rise to 25 and 700 respectively. Of 700 pupils, 57 were girls (3 belonging to Tripuri and 54 to Manipuri Community). But it was actually in 1894, a pathsala planned mostly for girls of high birth appeared at the desire of Maharani Tulsibati, a Manipuri scion which we have discussed earlier. But still the education for the hill people did not appear to become popular. In 1900-01 also, education was reported to be backward. From the beginning of the 20th century, education seemed to have begun among the hill people.

As the hill people's common economy depended on cultivation of jhum and the hard labour of it mostly rested on women folk, it was extremely hard to provide girls with education as they had to absent themselves away for a long time from household chores for this purpose; which a poor tribal family could hardly afford. This is the cause that despite the keen interest of the kings of Tripura for the development of education to some extent, the female education could not see the light of the day.

In 1935, according to No. 4 Memo of the Education Department in the stipend Exam, there is total discrimination in preparing the question paper for boys in the middle English and Higher Bengali, (the fees were 11/0, Lower Bengali and Patsala, 1/031) and for girls, the higher Bengali question paper has been prepared by 1/0. The most important point is that for girls there was no preparation of question paper for Middle English as the English teaching had not started for the girls.

It was only Maharaja Manikya Bahadur who first introduced the middle English among girls and also instructed if any girl wished to study higher English, she would be allowed to do so (1326 Edu. Rule). The Royal family girls and the same ranking elites get tuition of English privately which has its record in Tripura Gazette p. 233.

Government of Tripura,
Education Department,
No. 1699-1701 dt. 02. 05. 57 T.E.
5-10

Re: Appointment of Tutress to Maharaj Kumari

As desired by Her Highness Mata Maharani Mahadevi Mrs. P. Gupta is here by appointed Tutress to Maharaj Kumari on Rs 150/-(Rupees one hundred and fifty) P.M. plus an allowance of Rs 50/- (rupees fifty) P.M. She has joined her post on 1st of July last.

S.C. Dutta
Minister
Education Department.

In the year 1946, prior to the state's accession to the Indian Union, there were only 5 lower primary, 6 middle and one High English School for girls in the whole territory. The general trend was at that time on the level of just beginning and the much advanced plains people were gradually sending their girls to these schools but the tribal people of the hill areas were still in their slumber sleep. So the number of schools also extended like a slow coach. The total enrolment of girls students in the 4 primary schools at Agartala during the period was 1,026 only. But the post independence scenario of girls education was much more encouraging as there had been a very large scale increase of enrolment of girls student at all levels. Particularly at the primary level. By the end of the year 1963-64, the total number of students at the primary stage of all types of schools went well over 40,000. Facilities for girls' education had also been largely extended. All the primary and middle schools in this territory are mixed schools. Of the High Schools, 3 Multipurpose H. S. Schools, 7 class X High Schools and 3 Junior High Schools are exclusively meant for girls while 11 other Multipurpose H.S., 15 class X Schools and 31 Junior High Schools run co-educational classes.

Both the Colleges of this Territory were also co educational. The girls section of M.B.B. College opened in 1963-64and was subsequently turned to a full fledged women's College.

Not only that, to bring the awareness about the benefit of education particularly for girls, education of girls was made free in all schools of the territory. Girl students of S.T. and S.C. and O.B.C. are not charged tuition fee in the Government Colleges which also offer adequate hostel facilities to girl students of all communities. The S.T. and S.C. Girls get hostel facility without any cost. Moreover, now the Government has started periodical special coaching facilities after school hour for some important subjects like English, Science and Math up to class X level for the S.T. and S.C. students.

But to shift an agrarian old fashioned society to a developed educated one, where works other than cultivation are regarded as more handicap than as privilege as in the tribal society is an arduous task. The tribal women are the worst victim of it. In tribal societies of Tripura, though there is really no so called male dominance rather than a reasonable biological acceptance of the difference, which gives men and women clear cut economic functions, yet due to physical weakness than men, tribal women are submissive towards their men folk. But the tribal women are much more robust in health than their Bengali sibling sisters and this is the reason they have more power of endurance and resistance than the non tribal women to lead their lives without the least of minimum amenities. But their hard lives are much more free in some extent which even the so called sophisticated women of high class are denied. They don't bother in roaming anywhere, without restriction of time and without any 'veil' or 'parda'. The most modern approach of so called, educated aristocratic society's system can be found reflected in the custom of tribal marriage where a would be couple of the young girl and the boy live together separately from their families to cope up with the future marriage with more maturity and potentiality. Women are permitted to remarry after their widowhood or divorce. Socially though they are not allowed to become religious or non-religious leader, a tribal women's status, till today, particularly for educationally backward women, depends on the social position of her husband or father. Like women of almost any other patriarchal society of India, the tribal women also is protected by her father in childhood, in youth by her husband and in her old age by her son. It may be noted that at least on the field of marriage, the tribal women are little more at liberty, as the dowry problems don't bring them down into the position of a commodity. Though everything in the modern up to date world is saleable and the more elite the society is, the more expensive is the thing of sale whether it is skill or stamina, brain or strength, dignity or shrewdness, everything can be sold or purchased, only the language is different. And the bride of the marriage market of almost every society is the easy target to be bargained nakedly and openly. The tribal women are not still the prey of this modern world's ugly trap, on the contrary, to acquire bride in a tribal society, the bridegroom had to pay the bride price, which is really indicative of the higher social stand enjoyed by the tribal women. But as education, urbanization, modernization are gradually but steadily entering into the tribal society, the traditional and primitive qualities are also slowly loosening their grips to give birth to new curses into which the tribal women are also getting entangled. On the field of inheritance, the tribal women are losers. As descent is usually patrilineal, the sons alone inherit paternal property to the exclusion of daughters. Again influenced by the non tribal counterpart and modern outlook, many tribal societies, instead of bride price, demand dowry today though the economic participation of the tribal women is higher than that of their male counterparts. Though this is a new concerning trend and very limited miniscule numbers have joined into the fray, but the indication is not healthy for the tribal women.

In rural areas, particularly in remote and far flung areas, unmarried girls aged between 12 to 15 or 16 get busy in field work. These unmarried girls mostly drop out from primary level and are to look after not only field works but also other household work like helping in cooking, looking after brothers and sisters, sweeping, fetching water etc. Marriage for these girls does not bring any sort of difference or change in their life style. Marriage does not stand in the way of tribal women's participation in different activities like working on field or small scale industries or loom of their own huts. So economically large number of tribal women support themselves, and in their marital status, rural area based tribal women are much more supportive than those of the urban areas where only a few number of tribal women are equally economically supportive for doing any sort of manual work, particularly agriculture, which remains the single largest sector of employment for tribal women.

But though cultivation is the main source of income still today in tribal women's life in villages, the tribal women are not the land owners as a good number of customary law and tradition continue to be prevalent in tribal societies of Tripura. The tribal communities continue to be governed by unmodified customary law under which among patrilineal tribes, women's rights in land are severely circumscribed and typically limited to usufruct. So like patriarchal society, in tribal society also, it is the customary law that paternal property will go to son only and not to daughter. Here also, the tribal women are discriminated in regard to inheritance which shows the unequal social status of tribal women.

On agricultural front the tribal women perform almost 65 to 70 per cent work that include sowing, uprooting the seedlings, transplantation, weeding, harvesting, thrashing, yet for just gender bias, it is believed that without male participation and co-operation, tribal women are incapable of doing field work and most probably this is the reason, why the tribal women are not allowed to do the work of ploughing in the absence of male members, though the main work load rests on these women as the entire process of cultivation whether it is jhum or plain land, done entirely by tribal women. This purely manual labour without any outward tool rest on women folk.

Unequal payment for equal work is another discriminatory attitude towards the tribal women today in Tripura, not only between men and women but, it is there also between village and town, between younger tribal and tribal adult women. As poor landless tribal women are to accept this existing reality to support themselves in ardent poverty, though they are paid much less than men yet they are preferred for their doing work more sincerely and efficiently.

In the same way, though the tribal women involve in almost every household as well as outside work, yet in the share of any decision making whether on family basis or on community process, the tribal women are not allowed to take the decision single handedly. A similar conservative attitude towards tribal women is again shown on religious front also. They are not permitted to become the Chief of any religious organization or to perform any important religious rituals. Of course the wife of a religious Chief is highly regarded by the common mass which clearly indicates that individual identity of tribal women in almost all fields is minutely nil.

As Dr. Arunaday Saha, a regular columnist of the *Dainik Sambad*, the most widely circulated Bengali daily, wrote in one of his articles that women education is the best contraceptive for arresting population explosion and he nicely explained this theory economically also. Though the comment has been done somewhat humorously, the serious thought provoking and alarming idea lying underneath the jovial factor is absolutely true. If we analyze it methodically, we admit the fact and agree with him. Education has a positive impact upon the awareness about family planning because most of the tribal women particularly in remote villages and the far flung areas are still illiterate. Today's educated women hardly want to get married early or to invite double or triple children. Herein lies the special attention to be taken about the literacy level to assess the status of the tribal women before taking any steps towards family planning programme.

The age factor both for marriage and for steps taken in favour of family planning programme by the tribal women are significant. Most of the tribal women are still illiterate and have no formal education which is the main reason behind their non-acceptance of any family planning measures at their earlier stage of marriage. Before accepting any form of various medical or paramedical measures to restrict the size of the family, the numbers of new borns are already surpassed four to five. Lastly when the awareness comes, it is already too late to understand the ill effect of large family and poor socio- economic condition. Therefore, it is an established fact that education in the form of formal or non-formal whatever it may be, has a pivotal role in the acceptance of different family planning programmes.

The first Prime Minister of India, Pandit Jawaharlal Nehru proposed five principles for the welfare and development of the tribal communities. The first one is that (1) the tribals should develop along the line of their own genious, (2) that they must have their special rights in forest and land, (3) that a team of their own strained avoiding to prevent too many outside entries into tribal territory,(4) that over administration is to be avoided and non tribals should work in co-operation to their own cultural and social instructions and (5) that the money spent for them should not be counted instead stress should be given on the quality of human character evolved.

Other than these general five plans, the sixth plan stresses the need for the development work for the tribal women which are completely female oriented programmes.

The Seventh plan features different measures to give confidence among the tribal women, generate awareness about their rights and privileges and to train them for economic activity and employment. Access of women to land and have been proposed supporting through credit, marketing, training in management and technology. The use of technology minimize the scope of manpower and it displaces women workers in many fields. So this point is to be noted which is also suggested in the Seventh plan.

The technological upgradation of the production system creates unemployment and poverty that directly hit the women folk as the tribal women do almost all duties of household and play a great part in Jhuming and collection of forest products. So a major change in the methodology of planning should be done by less mechanized technique to raise employment for poorer section particularly for tribal women's employment. Accordingly, the Eighth plan has highlighted the development of women in general and the tribal women in particular. Thus a major change in the methodology of planning should be done for production of mass consumption goods by less mechanized technique to raise employment for poor tribal women to invite their self-confidence and respect within the household matters. The issues like land reform, distribution of surplus land both to the male and female, individual rights of land to women, changes in inheritance law in favour of the tribal women, resistance of social atrocities on women by landed gentry, removing of wage differential and to resist employment of tribal women in lower pay and legal help at hand should be done in such a way that these issues take a gradual change with the spread of education, modernization, liberalization, privatization and as well as nationalization. But it is impossible to do social justice without economic growth, particularly for weaker sections of women. Moreover, the weaker section's women particularly the tribal women adjusted more both for mental and vigorous physical strength in comparison with non-tribal women. One of the reasons may be access to government services and this requires minimum 10th standard education. But in forestry as well as in other small scale industries including cottage industry, a number of tribal women of both semi-literate and illiterate earn livelihood from these sources. The tribal women of the urban areas of Tripura are much more benefited both educationally and economically and thus obviously socially also. The urban tribal women are marching ahead with school, college and university degrees to fill up their quotas in every government and non government posts very fast which is surely a very encouraging trend to reflect a positive result on the status and empowerment of the tribal women of Tripura.

To make a total study of the status and empowerment of the tribal women of Tripura, a comparative survey of village versus town is done in taking the interviews of girls, all coming from remote areas to take the advantage of studying in good schools with free hostel facilities at Agartala and the women of highest official level, the completely advanced and well educated tribal established ladies. Let us listen from them how did they achieve their goals two to three decades before and what their ideas and thoughts about the present Tribal generation's advancement, specially the tribal women to acquire their destination, the desired status and empowerment to include themselves into the mainstream at per with the global women.

As already mentioned, the four communities have been taken into consideration namely the Tripuri, the Reang, the Jamatia and the Chakma and so girls and women from these four communities have been interviewed for our purposes. We will start from the Tripuri Community to discuss the position of their women reflecting the focus on educational, economical, social, marital, religious and inheritable ground.

The Tripuri Women

The Social Status

The status of any women in general is largely associated with the family she hails from. In the case of Tripuri women also, there is no exception. But a woman with fine qualities in her person and character can have a distinction of her own. The Tripuri women of the 21st century are proving this point slowly but steadily. According to J. Gon Choudhury, the status of the Tripuri women is somewhere between that of the Arunta women of East Africa and the Iroquoi women of upper New York. (A Corpus of Tripura). What he means to say is that present status of the Tripuri women is neither so free nor so conservative. It is neither so extremely open and flexible like western type nor so extremely orthodox or rigid like the Muslim type. The Tripuri women are assiduous and their position reminds us the valuable maxim the free is she who is more disciplined.

Through the life of a women in Tripuri society begins at home and ends at home, yet women with extra potentiality and other co-curricular activities take parts in different organizations to prove their skills and stamina. Both in rural and urban fronts, the Tripuri women almost outnumbered the other tribal women, in providing their qualities. It is also a fact that the Tripuri (3,30,872 in 1981, 461531 in 1991) constitute more than 50 per cent of the entire tribal population and though they have both rural and urban settlers their urban population is the highest of all tribes. So it is quite natural that the ratio of literacy, economic independence, developed social status and better category job are much higher in Tripuri women particularly living in urban area like Agartala.

The constitution of Independent India has given certain special benefits and provisions for rapid development of the backward communities. Accordingly the literacy rate shows steady rise since independence. Tripura's place in gaining literacy rate is much more remarkable comparing with other states of India and the S.T. and S.C have become considerably benefited by this programme. From the different table provided here it is proved that the Tripuri women have entered into almost every branch of education available. The Tripuri women with good qualities like teachers both in schools and colleges, efficient workers in the offices, dancers, singers, weavers and excellent folk lore tellers proved their worth not only on state level but some of them even on National level also.

The Tripuri are patriarchal and the lineage is traced through male members and hence they are also patrilineal. It is quite natural then that women do not enjoy the equal status as that of men. In their upbringing of children, the male child is given much indulgence while the girl child is not so much pampered. Her childhood ends sooner than her brother as domestic work load is placed on her shoulder. Outward activities specially in rural areas like collecting woods for fire, fetching water, sowing, weeding and harvesting are also expected from her. Though she is not put in restrictive clothing of parda but women are not allowed to take any major decisions, nor are they allowed to sell, purchase or mortgage lands. Thus the social status of Tripuri women is little lower rather than equal with men.

The Economic Status

Previously the whole Tripuri economy was hovering round agriculture and cultivation. In Jhuming generally, crops like paddy, cotton, maize are grown. But a tribal woman earns her own income by selling goats, fowls, pigs etc. and treats these as her own incomes which she keeps for herself. Thus in occupational pattern in the rural area, the picture has not changed much for the Tripuri women and agricultural sector remains almost the only source of occupation for them. The other source of income besides agriculture is the liquor brewing as the tribal people have the right to distil liquor in their indigenous process for consumption at home and within the community.

But the spread of literacy both in rural as well as urban areas among the Tripuri women, awakening the consciousness to continue their study as long as they can, made the literacy programmes of the Government and non-Government organization more or less fruitful and in the last decade of the last century, the Tripuri women who are more and more realizing the benefits of education, employment and economic independence, are carrying on their education up to University level to get settled with sound economic package. Thus the last decade presented many well educated Tripuri women who are economically well settled not only in educational department but also in many other departments which was unthinkable a few decades back. Thus economically, though few but the trend is encouraging, a Tripuri woman more or less, is enjoying an independent status, though not extensively.

The Marital Status

Though the tribal communities are much more liberal regarding free mixing of male and female, yet the Tripuri society does not permit free mixing of grown up boys and girls especially in interior regions. The advent of education is removing this inhibition gradually. The practice of bride price and marriage by service though apparently indicates at least a more dignified status of women, yet the real picture is something different. The modern educated bride groom does not agree to practice such primitive marriage ritual, instead demands huge dowry matching to his educational and economic status. The intention of marriage by service was to observe the future adjustment of the would be bride and groom which is now replaced in modern courtship like other societies. The Tripuri Community is also extremely fierce against any woman adultery whereas the same crime done by men is considered quite negligible and this attitude is absolutely the same like any other societies. But divorce is granted equally both to men and women on identical grounds like barrenness, impotency, adultery, insanity etc. Previously the female divorce rate was high whereas now a days the female divorce rate is much higher as female education made the economic independence possible in the Ttipuri women's lives. For the same reason, the Tripuri women are now more free to marry out of their class and to lead a life of their own choice.

The Tripuri women can have a share of their parental property but the amount is not equal to that of the male members of the family. The brothers are the greater beneficiaries in sharing the inheritance of property. From in laws portion after the husband's death, the wife can inherit it but not completely, as it is distributed among the children also in case of survival of children. With the rapid change of occupational pattern, more and more tribal men taking the tertiary occupations become the main bread earners of the family and women with little or not so good educational background can neither manage jobs nor can work on fields and naturally become dependent on their men. Taking the full advantage of this new condition, educated well employed grooms fetch dowry from bride's parents.

The Religious Status

The religious status of the Tripuri women is more or less like that of their Hindu sibling sisters. The women are not allowed to take any active participation in any religious ceremonies except some few rites in very few religious ceremonies like the 'Randhakmatai', and 'Chaklakmatai' etc. In matrimonial ceremonies, two women called 'Aiajuk' are required to be present in performing the rites. But the priesthood is totally a 'no zone' area for the women and here the complete male domination is found for doing every religious activities of the temple. In the famous temple of the tribals at old Agartala of the Chaudda Devta, for centuries, the chief priests and all other members of the temple are male Tripuries. In the same way the traditional village council is also formed only with the male members of each village as the Tripuri women are debarred to raise any voice or protest or to take any action against any male member. All these expose the monopoly of dominance of the male over the female, specially the religious status of the Tripuri women is strictly dominated by the male.

As the Constitution of India gives the equal right to each of its citizens, provides equal opportunities and forbids any differential treatment on grounds of sex, caste, creed etc., the tribal women and women of all other backward classes are benefited enormously. While the begining of the last century hardly produced any educated Tripuri women excepting a miniscule number in the Royal family, the end of the last century produced many educated Tripuri women with higher education and higher official posts which are really remarkable achievement on the part of these women. Though the condition of the Tripuri women varies from region to region, from village to town, from remote place to proper capital, yet the total outcome of this achievement of the Tripuri women is hopeful. Good education provides them good opportunity of well paid jobs which in turn will enhance the social and economic status of these women. A sound economic and educational status certainly ushers in a great empowerment and confidence with which the ability to change, to dictate or demand will grow to bring a beneficial balance in family, in community, in state and in nation. And that is the cherished goal and expected destination of women empowerment.

To show the educational as well as economic development of the Tripuri women particularly in last two to three decades, interviews of individual personalities have been taken on the women who are already empowered and some who are on the way of getting empowerment. The remarkable point to note is that the new generation of tribal women is much more outspoken in their thoughts and ideas which reflects their educated minds and developed upbringing. The already established tribal ladies who proved their potentialities on many fields, expressed their experiences and views on the given questions. Here are their minds.

A Sample Socio-economic and Educational Questionnarie-Cum-Interview of the Tripuri Women of Tripura.

Ouestionnaire A

1.	Name of the Town/ Village/Block/ Municipality/Panchayat	:	Kali Mohan Para, Jampuizalla
	District	:	Bhishalgarh, West Tripura
2.	Name of the Informant	:	TAPATI DEBBARMA
3.	Name of the Community	:	Tripuri, Tribe: Tribal of Tripura
4	Educational Qualification	:	Madhyamik, at present studying in class XI
5.	Present/Previous Working Status	:	Student
6.	Marital Status	:	Unmarried
7.	Social Activities, if any	:	No
8.	Economic Status (Present)	:	Cultivation.
9.	How many members of your family are literate	:	All the siblings (four).
10.	Elite Role:-		
	(a) Club	:	____
	(b) Library	:	Nil
	(c) Other prominent Committees	:	____

Ouestionnaire B

1. **What is your idea about the empowerment of women?**

Ans. The power of women.

2. **Do you feel that empowerment of women helps to achieve their desired status?**

Ans: Yes.

3. **How far these empowerment and status are achieved by the Tribal women of Tripura?**

Ans: Not so far.

4. **What plans and programmes do you think may be adopted by both the Central as well as the State Government to develop the status and Empowerment for the Tribal women of Tripura?**

Ans: The mass education for tribal women should be given the first priority by both the Governments introducing more facilities for them.

5. **Is there any distinction of treatment towards a boy child and a girl child in the Tribal society of Tripura?**

Ans: More or less the same.

6. **Would you like to study more and why?**

Ans: Yes, I would like to get higher studies to become economically well established.

7. **Is bride price practiced in your family?**

Ans: Yes.

8. **The dowry is also entering in your community. Would you support it?**

Ans: Absolutely not.

9. **How would you combat against this social curse?**

Ans: Self independence and self esteem of women may be the only answer to this problem.

10. **Any message for the new generation tribal from your side?**

Ans: Every tribal girls whether from village or town must get themselves educated.

Questionnaire A

1.	Name of the Town	:	Agartala
	District	:	West Tripura
2.	Name of the Informant	:	KARABI DEBBARMA
3.	Name of the Community	:	Tripuri, Tribe: SCHEDULED TRIBE
4	Educational Qualification	:	M.A., B.Ed.
5.	Present/Previous Working Status	:	Principal, Women's College (previously) Now Retired.
6.	Marital Status	:	Married
7.	Social Activities, if any	:	Many, Specially for Women & Red Cross Society
8.	Economic Status (Present)	:	Solvent
9.	How many members of your family are literate	:	Three
10.	Elite Role:-		
	(a) Club	:	yes
	(b) Library	:	yes
	(c) Other prominent Committees	:	yes

Questionnaire B

1. What is your idea about the empowerment of women?

Ans. To take their own decision single handedly and to materialize them successfully.

2. Do you feel that empowerment of women helps to achieve their desired status?

Ans: Yes. Self confidence with power brings this faith.

3. How far these empowerment and status are achieved by the Tribal women of Tripura?

Ans: It was unthinkable that common tribal girls were studying in schools 60 or 70 years back. Only some girls of the Royal tribal origin and aristocrat level sent their girls who used to go to M.T.B. Girls School accompanied by the female staff of the School as it was the only girls' school in Tripura at that time. There was a school bus for a very short period in which some girls of that time used to attend the school. But this was the picture of past. The present picture has been changed a lot. Yet the achievement to gain the desired status and empowerment by the tribal women of Tripura is a far cry.

4. **What plans and programmes do you think may be adopted by both the Central as well as the State Government to develop the status and Empowerment for the Tribal women of Tripura?**

Ans: I have stated many more times these issues in many seminars and workshops that education along with economic independence is the primary necessity for developing the status of the tribal women and therefore both the Governments, the state as well as the Central, should work keeping this point in their minds.

5. **Is there any distinction of treatment towards a boy child and a girl child in the Tribal society of Tripura?**

Ans: Not so far.

6 **Did you feel any discrimination while you pursue higher studies from your family or community?**

Ans: No. It is because perhaps our community is matriarchal.We are three brothers and five sisters all of whom were provided with education equally. We all are well established.

7. **What do you think the actual purpose of pursuing higher study for Tribal women should be -**

to manage a good career or to manage a high profiled husband or to do beneficial works for own community?

Ans: I got married before completion of my graduation and I completed my graduation and post graduation both after my marriage. So my higher study does not stand stall for my marriage. In my case, I managed everything - a good career, a high profiled husband and huge works not only for my own community but for everyone, specially for women and still today, in spite of my age, I try my best to continue my efforts.

8. **Women face insecurity, suppression, gender harassment in almost all male oriented places. Did you ever face such problems ?**

Ans: No. I was almost lone traveller on my own way. So no such feeling arises in my life.

9. **In what ways the much forwarded and well established Tribal women can contribute for the well being and prosperity of mass Tribal women of Tripura?**

Ans: As for myself, I threw myself to any sort of social work when necessary. I think I can set myself as an example to the women of new generation that at the age of more than 70, I am at service of social works.

10. **Any message for the new generation tribal from your side?**

Ans: In pursuing higher status and empowerment, women should not forget their humanity and feminity. The purpose of education is not only a good career, a comfortable and secured life but to become a total human being that can come for any use of this beautiful world.

Questionnaire A

1.	Name of the Town	:	Agartala
	District	:	West Tripura
2.	Name of the Informant	:	Smt. BITHIKA DEBBARMA
3.	Name of the Community	:	Tripuri, Tribe: SCHEDULED TRIBE
4	Educational Qualification	:	B.A.
5.	Present/Previous Working Status	:	Ex-member of Tripura Public Service Commission Previously Deputy Secretary of the Govt. of Tripura
6.	Marital Status	:	Unmarried
7.	Social Activities, if any	:	Member of the Tripura Adibasi Mahila Samiti.
8.	Economic Status (Present)	:	Independent
9.	How many members of your family are literate	:	All are literate
10.	Elite Role:-		
	(a) Club	:	____
	(b) Library	:	____
	(c) Other prominent Committees	:	Member of the Juvinile Board, Tripura

Questionnaire B

1. **What is your idea about the empowerment of women?**

Ans. I think empowerment of women should be Empowerment through proper mass education covering all walks of life, which will make women fit to realize the actual truth and take decision independently and freely for development of their own life.

2. **Do you feel that empowerment of women helps to achieve their desired status?**

Ans: Yes. The educated women will be able to contribute for advancement of the society according to their merit and such contribution will automatically provide a respectable place in the society.

3. **How far these empowerment and status are achieved by the Tribal women of Tripura?**

Ans: Nothing notable.

4. **What plans and programmes do you think may be adopted by both the Central as well as the State Government to develop the status and Empowerment for the Tribal women of Tripura?**

Ans: The Central as well as the State Government simultaneously should take immediate steps to arrange for mass education of Tribal women of Tripura.

5. **Is there any distinction of treatment towards a boy child and a girl child in the Tribal society of Tripura?**

Ans: Though the boy child is regarded as a scion but the girl child also is not neglected.

6. **Did you feel any discrimination while you pursue higher studies from your family or community?**

Ans: No.

7. **What do you think the actual purpose of pursuing higher study for Tribal women should be - to manage a good career or to manage a high profiled husband or to do beneficial works for own community?**

Ans: To do beneficial works not only for own community but also for mankind as a whole.

8. **Women face insecurity, suppression, gender harassment in almost all male oriented places. What is your opinion and suggestions?**

Ans: Educated conscious women are likely to be able to tackle such problems. But most worst gender harassment which women always are to face is rape.The Government and we all women and all men together should try to find out a path to save women from such heinous harassment.

9. In what ways the much forwarded and well established Tribal women can contribute for the well being and prosperity of mass Tribal women of Tripura?

Ans: Anybody if desires,may contribute for the uplift of the Tribal women of Tripura through N.G.O s and other societies etc. functioning for welfare of the communities.

10. Any message for the new generation tribal from your side?

Ans: Education is the key to prosperity of each and all. So educate yourselves firstly.

Questionnaire A

1.	Name of the Town	:	Agartala
	District	:	West Tripura
2.	Name of the Informant	:	Dr. PANCHALI DEBBARMA
3.	Name of the Community	:	Tripuri, Tribe: Tribal of Tripura
4	Educational Qualification	:	M.B.B.S.
5.	Present/Previous Working Status	:	Medical Officer, I.G.M. Hospital (THS) Grade-IV
6.	Marital Status	:	Married
7.	Social Activities, if any	:	Yes, (three medical aid)
8.	Economic Status (Present)	:	Independent
9.	How many members of your family are literate	:	All are literate

10. Elite Role:-
    (a) Club : ____
    (b) Library : ____
    (c) Other prominent Committees : ____

Questionnaire B

1. **What is your idea about the empowerment of women?**

Ans: Women are considered to be the weaker sex by majority of humanity in our society. Hence their status lies suppressed in most parts of the world specially in India- where, ironically women power is worshipped in form of the mother Goddess and where all beautiful serene essential resources in the country and the universe are referred to admiringly as females - for example Earth, River, Nature, Energy are all referred as the Mother Earth, the Mother Ganga, etc. It is high time that women are liberated from a confined livelihood and empowered with various abilities for the benefit of themselves as well as for the benefit of the whole society because it is a fact that 'the hand that rocks a cradle rules the World', as women are powerful endorsed with many potentialities which the society fails to acknowledge.

2. **Do you feel that empowerment of women helps to achieve their desired status?**

Ans: Yes, indeed. Empowerment is the only way to make the women to reach their desired status.

3. **How far these empowerment and status are achieved by the Tribal women of Tripura?**

Ans: The empowerment of Tribal women of Tripura has achieved a welcomingly considerable extent in the present age where the tribal women who were previously looking after their families and fields are now shining in all fields of knowledge and profession lending their potentialities as great musicians, officers, architects, doctors, journalist, artists,athletes and in also fashion skills and beauty pageants.

4. **What plans and programmes do you think may be adopted by both the Central as well as the State Government to develop the status and Empowerment for the Tribal women of Tripura?**

Ans: Both Central and the State Government should adapt measures to fully utilize the abilities of the tribal women. Lending educational benefits and facilities along with the spreading of message of educational need to the remote Tribal societies would help so that the purpose of educational status of women is clearly understood by them. Trained fields works should be employed in the remote areas to explain and convince the public about the uplift of women with message of new ideas, self acquired income and respectable jobs in all fields. Tribal women should be encouraged to serve in panchyats, in voluntary organizations working for the uplift of women. It should be borne in mind that the proposed 'Inner line' action plans would be a disastrous step- as it would seal off the roads of learning from the outside world. Women should be encouraged with financial assistance to travel in groups to other states and countries to observe as well as to compete with their counterparts outside their own state. This would help them acknowledge the status of women in those states and kindle a quest to learn cottage industries employing women would help to retrieve them of their economical burdens.

5. **Is there any distinction of treatment towards a boy child and a girl child in the Tribal society of Tripura?**

Ans: There is the distinction of treatment towards a boy child and a girl in certain remote areas of Tribal population in Tripura. But in urban areas it is not the case.

6. **Did you feel any discrimination while you pursue higher studies from your family or community?**

Ans: No.

7. **What do you think the actual purpose of pursuing higher study for Tribal women should be - to manage a good career or to manage a high profiled husband or to do beneficial works for own community?**

Ans: The actual purpose of achieving higher status and study in tribal women should be to bring about benefits for the self as well as to our community around us.

8. **Women face insecurity, suppression,gender harassment in almost all male oriented places. What is your opinion and suggestions?**

Ans: Insecurity, suppression and gender harassments of women in male oriented places should be abolished with the help of a stern administrative policy laid down rules that would make these acts punishable under law and also by educating society about the advantages of women empowerment in this age-when women could share the burden of men to up bring families and societies with the help of their own uplift.

9. **In what ways the much forwarded and well established Tribal women can contribute for the**

well being and prosperity of mass Tribal women of Tripura?

Ans: It would bring about 'awareness' amidst the Tribal women population in Tripura which would lead to brilliant aspects of prosperity to the Tribal Women of Tripura would then become standing examples to their counterparts all over the world.

10. Any message for the new generation tribal from your side?

Ans: The message that comes from the bottom of my heart would echo in all Tribal women's hearts and it would be as follows:—

Arm yourself with knowledge, Education, utilize the resources lent by the Central and State Government to attain a perfect secured livelihood that would enlighten and benefit self, the immediate kith and kin and also the societies around you to live in comfort and glory and at the same time passing the message and glory to our future budding generations who would instill many more modern ideas to gloritfy our humble presence here in our mother land—Jai Hind.

Questionnaire A

1.	Name of the Town	:	Agartala
	District	:	West Tripura
2.	Name of the Informant	:	SOBHA DEBBARMA
3.	Name of the Community	:	Tripuri, Tribe: SCHEDULED TRIBE
4	Educational Qualification	:	M.Sc.
5.	Present/Previous Working Status	:	Principal, Women's College Govt. of Tripura, At present Inspector of College, Tripura University

6. Marital Status : Widow
7. Social Activities, if any : ______
8. Economic Status (Present) : Solvent
9. How many members of your family are literate : Three
10. Elite Role:-
   (a) Club : ____
   (b) Library : ____
   (c) Other prominent Committees : ____

Questionnaire B

1. **What is your idea about the empowerment of women?**

Ans: To become Empowered,Women should prepare themselves to remain empowered.

2. **Do you feel that empowerment of women helps to achieve their desired status?**

Ans: Yes.

3. **How far these empowerment and status are achieved by the Tribal women of Tripura?**

Ans: Not so far.

4. What plans and programmes do you think may be adopted by both the Central as well as the State Government to develop the status and Empowerment for the Tribal women of Tripura?

Ans: **Improvement of Education system and improvement of economic status.**

5. Is there any distinction of treatment towards a boy child and a girl child in the Tribal society of Tripura?

Ans: Not so far.

6. **Did you feel any discrimination while you pursue higher studies from your family or community?**

Ans: No.

7. **What do you think the actual purpose of pursuing higher study for Tribal women should be - to manage a good career or to manage a high profiled husband or to do beneficial works for own community?**

Ans: For self conscious, self elevation and to help the society and community.

8. **Women face insecurity,suppression,gender harassment in almost all male oriented places. What is your opinion and suggestions?**

Ans: It varies from place to place.Self consciousness is necessary.

9. **In what ways the much forwarded and well established Tribal women can contribute for the well being and prosperity of mass Tribal women of Tripura?**

Ans: Awareness campaign.

10. **Any message for the new generation tribal from your side?**

Ans: Educate and let them educate, think properly and widely.

Questionnaire A

1.	Name of the Town	:	Agartala
	District	:	West Tripura
2.	Name of the Informant	:	MANIDIPA DEBBARMA
3.	Name of the Community	:	Tripuri, Tribe: TRIPURI
4	Educational Qualification	:	M.Sc. (PHYSICS)
5.	Present/Previous Working Status	:	State Government Service, Principal, Netaji Subhas Mahavidhyalaya, Udaipur, At present Principal, Govt. Women College, Agartala

6.	Marital Status	:	Married
7.	Social Activities, if any	:	Nothing worth mentioning.
8.	Economic Status (Present)	:	Independent.
9.	How many members of your family are literate	:	All are literate.
10.	Elite Role:-		
	(a) Club	:	____
	(b) Library	:	____
	(c) Other prominent Committees	:	Syndicate Member of Tripura University.

Questionnaire B

1. **What is your idea about the empowerment of women?**

Ans: Empowerment of women is a pre-condition for their all round development and elevation of their social status.

2. **Do you feel that empowerment of women helps to achieve their desired status?**

Ans: Yes. It contributes largely not only in individual cases but has also a positive effect on the women in general to achieve their desired status.

3. **How far these empowerment and status are achieved by the Tribal women of Tripura?**

Ans: They are lagging far behind if compared with the female members of the advanced societies. The reason may be attributed primarily to their deficiency in the academic fields and partly to their impoverished condition.

4. **What plans and programmes do you think may be adopted by both the Central as well as the State Government to develop the status and Empowerment for the Tribal women of Tripura?**

Ans: Setting up of large number of girls' schools in the interior areas with free boarding and lodging facilities and side by side to ensure the self employment of the Tribal women in the field of handicrafts, weavings and other small scale Cottage Industries are required. Simultaneously to develop the overall standard of the tribal women. The State and Central Govternment should ensure marketing of the finished products of the Tribal women.

5. **Is there any distinction of treatment towards a boy child and a girl child in the Tribal society of Tripura?**

Ans: No.

6. **Did you feel any discrimination while you pursue higher studies from your family or community?**

Ans: No.

7. **What do you think the actual purpose of pursuing higher study for Tribal women should be - to manage a good career or to manage a high profiled husband or to do beneficial works for own community?**

Ans: The primary object of Higher study should be to contribute to the uplift of the Tribal Society as a whole. The other purpose of managing a good career or a high profiled husband will be fulfilled as a natural corollary.

8. **Women face insecurity, suppression, gender harassment in almost all male oriented places. What is your opinion and suggestions?**

Ans: Extensive co-education *and* social awareness in the proper direction appear to be of great importance.

9. **In what ways the much forwarded and well established Tribal women can contribute for the**

well being and prosperity of mass Tribal women of Tripura?

Ans: The established Tribal women in batches may organize zonal seminars and group meetings for interaction with the backward tribal women frequently.

10. Any message for the new generation tribal from your side?

Ans: They should consider them as identical with and part and parcel of any other Indian societies at the national level. They should also be diligent and persuasive to achieve the goal.

After the Tripuri Community, the Reang Community comes the next in numerical strength. We will discuss the position of women of this Community in the same way like the Tripuri.

Questionaire-A

1.	Name of the Town	:	Agartala
	District	:	West Tripura
2.	Name of the Informant	:	Miss Suniti Deb Barman
3.	Name of the Community	:	Tripuri Tribe: Tribal of Tripura
4.	Eduactional Qualification	:	B.A., B.Ed.
5.	Persent/Previous Working Status	:	1. Captain lady officer of NCC, 71, Tripura Girls Independent Company, wef 23.03.1966 to 31.5.1976 2. Chief Superintendent of Protective Home, Taranagar, Mohanpur, Wef. 1986 to 1997 Retired as Grade A Gazetted Officer.
6.	Marital Status	:	Single, Unmarried.

7.	Social Activities, if any	:	Secretary, Nikhil Tripura Mahila Manch. Member of Tripura Adbashi Mahila Samity. Member of Kalyan Samity, Member of Board of Visitors Health and Family Welfare Department, Agartala, Govt., of Tripura.
8.	Economic Status (Present)	:	Retired Grade 'A' Gazetted Officer.
9.	How many members of your family are literatre	:	Eight (8) nos.
10.	Elite Role	:	
	(a) Club	:	
	(b) Library	:	Birchandra Public Library, Agartala, Tripura.
	(c) Other prominent Committees	:	Kastoora Gandhi Smarak Samity.

Questionaire-B

1. What is your idea about the empowerment women?

Ans. Empowerment of women is necessary in all respects for the progress in any every movement, i.e., Social economical and educational for the women of the nation.

2. Do you feel that empowerment of women helps to achieve their desire status?

Ans. Empowerment is the key to achieve status in the society as well as globaly.

3. How far these empowerment and status are achieved by the Tribal women of Tripura?

Ans. These empowerment and status may be achieved by the Tribal women of Tripura by proper education, Social concern and positive attitude among the Tribal women of Tripura.

4. **What plans and programmes do you think may be adopted by both the Central as well as the State Government to develop the status and Empowerment for the Tribal women of Tripura?**

Ans. Both the Central and State Government should give various facilities such as free eduction, vocational training, granting of scholarship to the meritorius students, providing hostels for the students studing at various schools and colleges at Agartala apart from the students residing at Agartala.

5. **Is there any distinction of treatment towards a boy child and a girl child in the Tribal society of Tripura?**

Ans. No, there is not any distinction between a boy and child a girl child in the Tribal society of Tripura.

6. **Did you feel any discrimination while your pursue higher studies from your family or community?**

Ans. No, I did not feel any discimination while persuing higher studies.

7. **What do you think the actual purpose of pursuing higher study for the Tribal women should be—to manage a good career or to manage a high profiled husband or to do beneficial works for own community?**

Ans. Pursuing higher study I personaly feel that I can manage a good career, achieve a higher status in the society. I am economically independent enough so I can help lots of other under privileged people of my own community. I can help uneducated one with my knowledge and my social concern.

8. **Women face insecurity, suppression, gender**

harassment in almost all male oriented places. What is your opinion and suggestions?

Ans. Yes, off course women face insecurity, suppression, gender harassment in almost all male oriented places. But we should also not forget that Late Indira Gandhi, Late Kalpana Chawla and Kiran Bedi have gone beyond all these and proved themselves higher in every respect in all male oriented places.

9. **In what ways the much forwarded and well established Tribal women can contribute for the well being and prosperity of mass Tribal women of Tripura?**

Ans. The much forwarded and well established Tribal women should aware the Tribal women about illiteracy, early marriage, superstition, the concern of health and family welfare.

10. **Any message for the new generation tribal from your side?**

Ans. Lastly, but not leastly my message for the new generation Tribal is make yourselves educated enough so you can enlighten others. Have positive attitude, reach the sky in every respect be it sports, arts, culture. Make Tripura reacher in socioeconomically. Contribute to the people of the nation so, it can make itself advance in prospective ways. Also, try and help in national integrity. Try to live in peace brotherhood and love.

The Reang Women

The Social Status

In numerical strength, the Reangs are the second largest community of Tripura's tribal society. Almost in all sub-division, they have settled but in Dharmanagar and Amarpur, they are found in thick population. From 1961 to 1981, their population increased from 56,597 to 85,836. In literacy rate, the Reangs are lagging behind and the women education is more negligible. Recently a miniscule number of the Reang women are coming out in different higher Government and non-Government posts armed with college and university education. Socially, the Reangs are also patriarchal in nature as the head of the family gets enough authority and regards from other members of the family. The women folk do every household works including outside cultivation. Liquor making is controlled by the Reang women, as it is believed that if a man brews, the liquor will lose its proper taste. In rural areas, like all other tribal women, the Reang women also do almost the same work from dawn to dusk to keep her family intact. But though she shares all works equally with male members, yet her social status is much lower than her male counterpart as she is.debarred from making any decision or any authority.

Economic Status

The economic status of the Reang women is very unpredictable as educationally they are not sound enough. Their principal demands are fulfilled from the forest resources and the primitive method of cultivation of Jhum is their main source of economy still today. Other sources are hunting, fishing, collecting jungle products etc. But with the fast deforestation and the Govternment's policy of forest acquisition, the Reang women are facing great difficulty to meet their requirements. The landless women are the poorest of the poor who work as daily labour on other's land and are exploited readily as the rate of wage of women labours is less than male labour though the women labourers work with much sincerity. Those few who managed good education are economically sound but their number is awfully meagre.

The Marital Status

The marital status of the Reang women is alike or the Tripuris, the Jamatias, the Noatias, and the Uchais as pre-marital chastity are not a matter of serious concern. In Captain Lewin's words 'great freedom of intercourse is allowed among the puran Tipperahs, Noatias, Jamatias, Reangs and Uchais of the Chittagong Hill Tracts' (Lewin, Capt T.H. : THE HILL TRACTS OF CHITTAGONG AND DWELLERS THERE IN Calcutta- 1869). Like all other tribal communities, the Reang women can get married by marriage of service, marriage of bride price, by exchange etc. Though the traditional means of marriage by rendering physical services is now fast receding among the educated grooms. With a change in the means and mode of production and livelihood, the relative position of brides and grooms is going to be altered. The gradual loss of main economic contribution of women with the cultivated lands and other forest products, a new change and a challenge are slowly invading the tribal women's world also. The marriage by service and by bride price are subsiding with dowry system.

In the Reang women's life, divorce is permissible on the common grounds like others tribal communities but like Achilles heel, the sore point lies in the fact that no divorce can be legally valid unless the husband consents to it. So here at least, the marital status of the Reang women is much more lower than that of their other tribal sibling sisters.

The Religious Status

Through urbanization, the penetration of modern economy, education and administrative machinery, the democratic concept of the welfare state have definitely broken the stagnation and isolation to usher in a new light that has removed many superstitious beliefs of meaningless dreaded rituals in the Reang society. Yet some religious rituals are there that are mostly under the command of the men folk as their priest along with other associates relating to religious activities are all men where women are hardly allowed. Not only this, the Reangs administrative heads and the pivotal place of the Sardar or Chief are all strictly men members reducing the religious status of the Reang women who can not take any authoritarian position for any ritual whether it is birth or marriage or death.

Thus the Reang community is lagging behind and therefore the women's development on almost every field is extremely low. It is estimated that 85 per cent of the Reang community may be considered as P.G.P. considering the snail speeded progress of their development. A Separate Directorate of Tribal Rehabilitation in plantation and Primitive Group Programme (T.R.P. and P.G.P.) was created by the Govt. of Tripura for the development of this Primitive tribe. A separate corporation which is known as T.R.P.C. is functioning for rehabiliation of tribals through rubber based settlement programmes.

As we have taken the interviews of the Tripuri women studying in schools, colleges and the university and also of some established ladies, in the same way,the interviews of the Reahg women are listed below:

Questionnaire A

1.	Name of the Village/ Panchayat/Sub-Division	:	Karbuk Nabajoy Para, Amarpur. South District.
2.	Name of the Informant	:	Chintarong Reang.
3.	Name of the Community	:	Reang, Tribe: SCHEDULED TRIBE
4	Educational Qualification	:	Class X Standard
5.	Present/Previous Working Status	:	Student

6.	Marital Status	:	Unmarried
7.	Social Activities, if any	:	Nil
8.	Economic Status (Present)	:	Dependent
9.	How many members of your family are literate	:	Seven except parents
10.	Elite Role:-		
	(a) Club	:	____
	(b) Library	:	____
	(c) Other prominent Committees	:	____

Questionnaire B

1. **What is your idea about the empowerment of women?**

Ans: I have no clear idea of it.

2. **At what age did you start your study?**

Ans: At the age of 8.

3. **How far these empowerment and status are achieved by the Tribal women of Tripura?**

Ans: As I have already mentioned that I have no proper idea, but this much I can say that girls like me from villages are now much interested in study.

4. **Why have you come to study at Agartala ?**

Ans: To take the facility of a good school and free girls' hostel.

5. **Would you like to study more ?**

Ans: Yes. I have come to Agartala to get the facility of higher education to make myself well established.

6. **What is your father's profession ?**

Ans: Cultivation.

7. **Do all the girls of your village like the same profession of your father go to school ?**

Ans: No. Not all but almost everyone want to study at the town. As my situation permits, I have come Agartala to study.

8. **Is bride price practiced in your family ? what is your opinion about it?**

Ans: Yes. I support it.

9. **How do you support the new entry of dowry system in your community ?**

Ans: Absolutely not.

10. **How would then combat against this social curse ?**

Ans: Girl's education can fight it back.

Questionaire A

1.	Name of the Village/ Block/Sub-Division	:	Baxmichara/Bagafa South Belonia.
2.	Name of the Informant	:	Lipika Reang.
3.	Name of the Community	:	Reang, Tribe: Tribal of Tripura
4	Educational Qualification	:	M.A. in Pol. Science.
5.	Present/Previous Working Status	:	Nil
6.	Marital Status	:	Unmarried
7.	Social Activities, if any	:	Yes
8.	Economic Status (Present)	:	Dependent
9.	How many members of your family are literate	:	All are literate. Both the parents are service holder.
10.	Elite Role:-		
	(a) Club	:	——
	(b) Library	:	——
	(c) Other prominent Committees	:	——

Questionnaire B

1. **What is your idea about the empowerment of women?**

Ans. "Empowerment of women", means the power of the women for almost all things.

2. **Do you feel that empowerment of women helps to achieve their desired status?**

Ans: Yes, I do believe so.

3. **How far these empowerment and status are achieved by the Tribal women of Tripura?**

Ans: Though general condition was not entirely favourable, still it was not unsatisfactory to prosecute study.

4. **What plans and programmes do you think may be adopted by both the Central as well as the State Government to develop the status and Empowerment for the Tribal women of Tripura?**

Ans: There are already some plans and programmes but the proper uses and materialization of them should be done.

5. **Is there any distinction of treatment towards a boy child and a girl child in the Tribal society of Tripura?**

Ans: No, I don't think so.

6. **Did you feel any discrimination while you pursue higher studies from your family or community?**

Ans: No, I didn't.

7. **What do you think the actual purpose of pursuing higher study for Tribal women should be - to manage a good career or to manage a high profiled husband or to do beneficial works for own community?**

Ans: First to manage a good career then naturally that will manage other things also.

8. Women face insecurity,suppression,gender harassment in almost all male oriented places. What is your opinion and suggestions?

Ans: Sometimes women themselves invite these. Good personality, self dignity, command on works help to keep these menaces at bay.

9. In what ways the much forwarded and well established Tribal women can contribute for the well being and prosperity of mass Tribal women of Tripura?

Ans: There are so many ways but the real willingness to do something and not just preaching, attending meetings and seminars can contribute few things towards this goal.

10. Any message for the new generation tribal from your side?

Ans: They should follow up the paths of the educated and empowered tribal women for uplift in all fields. We have to fight for legal, educational, economic, political, social and cultural rights. Our due rights must be fulfilled. Only slogan is not the practical remedy. Sincerity, co-operation, efficiency, working ability, impartial outlook etc., may keenly be followed.

Questionnaire A

1.	Name of the Town	:	Vill: East Bagafa, Radha Kishoreganj Block
	Sub-Division	:	Belonia, District: Tripura South
2.	Name of the Informant	:	Miss. Saihdeivung (jule) Reang. Age-23

3.	Name of the Community	:	Reang, Tribe: Scheduled Tribe
4	Educational Qualification	:	M.A. (Part-II) Student in Pol. Science. (Tripura University)
5.	Present/Previous Working Status	:	Nil
6.	Marital Status	:	Unmarried
7.	Social Activities, if any	:	Yes I take part in social activities
8.	Economic Status (Present)	:	Father-Dy. Collector, D.M's Office, West Tripura.
9.	How many members of your family are literate	:	Male-2, Female - 4 (Total Six) 1 Brother M.B.B.S. (1st year), 3 sisters, 1 M.A. (2nd Year), 1 B.A. (1st year) and another class XI in Arts Stream.
10.	Elite Role:-		
	(a) Club	:	____
	(b) Library	:	____
	(c) Other prominent Committees	:	____

Questionnaire B

1. **When did you first start your study?**

Ans. 1983-1984

2. **What was the general condition of girls particularly the tribal girls who wanted to study at that time?**

Ans: Though general condition was not entirely favourable, still it was not unsatisfactory to prosecute study.

3. **How far these empowerment and status are achieved by the Tribal women of Tripura?**

Ans: Not so far.

4. **What plans and programmes do you think may be adopted by both the Central as well as the State Government to develop the status and Empowerment for the Tribal women of Tripura?**

Ans: The mass education for tribal women should be given the first priority by both the Governments introducing more facilities for them.

5. **Is there any distinction of treatment towards a boy child and a girl child in the Tribal society of Tripura?**

Ans: Today no one think about it so seriously.

6. **Would you like to study more and why?**

Ans: Yes, I would like to get higher studies to become economically well established.

7. **How far the status and empowerment of the tribal women have reached the final goal ?**

Ans: Truly speaking, not up to the mark at all.

8. **The dowry is entering in your community. Would you support it?**

Ans: Absolutely not.

9. **How would you combat against this social curse?**

Ans: Self independence and self esteem of women may the only answer to this problem.

10. **Any message for the new generation tribal from your side?**

Ans: Every tribal girls whether from village or town must get themselves educated. Our due rights must be fulfilled. Demand for equal status and right in the practical field must be done in the Government level as well as the social level. Practical programmes and schemes should be chalked out from Government organization relating to tribal women.

Questionnaire A

1.	Name of the Town	:	Agartala
	District	:	West Tripura
2.	Name of the Informant	:	Dr. BASANTI REANG
3.	Name of the Community	:	Reang, Tribe: Scheduled Tribe
4	Educational Qualification	:	M.B.B.S.
5.	Present/Previous Working Status	:	As J.M.O. Narsingarh, PHC Tripura(W)
6.	Marital Status	:	Unmarried
7.	Social Activities, if any	:	Attached with SSH (Short Stay Home) Natunnagar, Airport Road, A,NGO.
8.	Economic Status (Present)	:	Solvent and Independent
9.	How many members of your family are literate	:	All are literate. Father expired as ex-serviceman Mother still in service in C.I.B in Social Education Department. Brother Medical, Engineer Sister-M.B.B.S.
10.	Elite Role:-		
	(a) Club	:	____
	(b) Library	:	____
	(c) Other prominent Committees	:	____

Questionnaire B

1. **What is your idea about the empowerment of women?**

Ans. "Empowerment of women", means- the power of the women to judge the good or bad, right or wrong, the power to take decisions, the total freedom,where she can think freely, she can move fearless, without any kind of suppression,and with her head high in the society.

2. **Do you feel that empowerment of women helps to achieve their desired status?**

Ans: Yes, I do believe so.

3. **How far these empowerment and status are achieved by the Tribal women of Tripura?**

Ans: If, we think about the total women-population of Tripura - a very small part of it is educated and has seen the light of civilization. The major chunk of it is still living in the darkness of ignorance, social barriers and poverty. So I think the so called empowerment and status are yet to be achieved by the Tribal women of Tripura. There is a long way to go for them.

4. **What plans and programmes do you think may be adopted by both the Central as well as the State Government to develop the status and Empowerment for the Tribal women of Tripura?**

Ans: Regarding the plans and programmes - if ever to be adopted by the state as well as Central Government to develop the status and empowerment for the Tribal women of Tripura - should be by:-

(a) Provision of more Educational scopes especially for those, who are living in the far remote, interiors of the state.

(b) Providing proper rehabilitation-oriented schemes for the school drop outs, so that they can think about their next generations and take the further essential steps.

(c) Making the Rural women economically stronger

and independent by making them more interested to participate in the various opportunities provided by the State and Central Government, e.g. various small scale industries/business schemes through various advertisements, or direct approaches to them through the panchayats villages - leaders or the organization working under the guidance of State or Central Government.

5. **Is there any distinction of treatment towards a boy child and a girl child in the Tribal society of Tripura?**

Ans: No, I don't think so.

6. **Did you feel any discrimination while you pursue higher studies from your family or community?**

Ans: No, I didn't.

7. **What do you think the actual purpose of pursuing higher study for Tribal women should be-to manage a good career or to manage a high profiled husband or to do beneficial works for own community?**

Ans: I think it would be to manage a good career and to do beneficial works not only for own community but for the whole mankind.

8. **Women face insecurity, suppression, gender harassment in almost all male oriented places. What is your opinion and suggestions?**

Ans: My opinion regarding the matter is - there should be a complete change or rather, we should learn to change the customs and practices in our society. In large sense, every family is the unit of the whole society. In this sense, what we are doing in our family is reflected in our society. Hence we should learn to take good and proper care of a girl child/women in our family or society,vice versa.

9. In what ways the much forwarded and well established Tribal women can contribute for the well being and prosperity of mass Tribal women of Tripura?

Ans: There are so many ways for this purpose - but basically, one should be well determined,strong headed, and very patient to influence the mass, being a role model to them. Secondly one should participate in various developmental activities in different fields like education, rehabilitation, socio-economic grounds etc. providing the mass with various information regarding the developments and achievements of women from other parts of the country and world through group discussions, seminars meetings establishing various organizations for all these purposes.

10. Any message for the new generation tribal from your side?

Ans: My messages are that-there are so many changes and opportunities in our lives-so every life should be started with an aim. One should dare to dream and work hard to achieve that and there is no alternative but to work hard.

The Jamatia Women

The Social Status

The Jamatias are another important tribal community of Tripura. Like the Tripuris or the Reangs, they don't have any subdivision or sub class in their community. The Jamatia society is strictly patriarchal, the system which they call 'Santai' and therefore men are more powerful in taking any authoritarian decision. But in sharing work either on field or any household work, the Jamatia women play the key role. In the traditional Jamatia society, as in all other hill people of Tripura, the predominant mode of productive activity is Jhuming in which the active participation of women is essential. Besides this, husking rice, extracting oil from oil seeds, collecting fire wood, fetching water, feeding pigs and poultry and carding cotton are the female domain. Brewing liquor is also the only field where the Jamatia women are excellent which they prepare themselves in their own houses. So the Jamatia women are hard workers giving much more labour than the men yet their status is recognized by the status of their husbands. They never challenge the superiority of the men. They are not permitted to take part in village council elections. They are not eligible for the pose of 'Chowdhuri' Meyal Sardar or Hada okra on the plea that the womenfolk are not well acquainted with social rules and regulations. Dr. (Mrs.) Chandrika Basu (Majumdar) Reader and H.O.D., Deptt. of Political Science, Tripura University observed that Hada okra's wife is honoured and enjoys special prestige in the Society.

The Marital Status

The Jamatia women enjoy much freedom before her marriage by spending a customary period with her would be partner for a matured outcome of marriage. She has the right to divorce, remarriage on widowhood and to choose her own life partner. But the rule of polyandry in which a woman can marry more than one husband is strictly prohibited for a Jamatia woman whereas though very rarely the men can marry more than one woman. In marriage system, there is one restrictive rule both for the Jamatia men and women. Under this rule, a widower can not marry any spinster, if he wishes to remarry, he has to marry a widow only. The same rule is provided for the women also. The trial marriage system or 'Jamaikhata' is fast receding and, the system of bride price is still prevalent in this society.

The Economic Status

As the Jamatia women are extremely hardworking and contribute huge hard labour equally on outside front as well as inside front, the economic status of the Jamatia women is much important in the economic sphere of the family. In Jamatia society, the economic sphere is divided almost equally both between men and women as women share every work, sometimes the burden of work left more on women's shoulder. Though on economic ground, there is no such thing as male dominance, yet a reasonable biological acceptance is taken mutely by the women on the basis of superior physical strength of the men. In the Jamatia society, the rule of inheritance is the law of equigeniture as the women can inherit property. The women have the right in father's property.

Father's Property

Dr. K.B. Jamatia, Deputy Registrar, Tripura University, has elaborately discussed the economic status of Jamatia women in his their entitled the Jamatias of Tripura–A Historical study (1863-1965). The Jamatia women help their men in various agricultural works like weeding, transplanting, harvesting, etc. As a matter of fact, there is no dominant role of the male rather a division of labour exist.

According to K.B. Jamatia

The earlier division of labour was mostly based on shifting cultivation. Today, shifting cultivation is no more. The women are also becoming educated. There are engineers, doctors and teachers among the Jamatia women today. They now vie with their men counterparts for jobs and social honours. During this process of change in their status, they were and are still left behind the wallow in the mire of deprived status. Hence, as Elaine Morgan has pointed out the women will have to be united in order to earn their due place in the society."

Varrier Elwin observed that, "For a tribal family, to send its grown up girl or boy to a school, is essentially a matter of economics; and entails dislocation in the traditional pattern of division of labour... many parents can not just afford to send their children to school."

The Educational Status

Dr. K.B. Jamatia reported that the first school was established in 1947 by the leaders of Jana Sikha movement in the areas of Jamatia. Primary education rapidly developed with the establishment of educational institution in the Jamatia dominated villages like Noabari, Pitra, Bagma, Shilghati, Tutabari. Before 1950, there was not a graduate of this community. Dr. Jamatia has conducted a survey which is shown in this table.

Distribution of Jamatia Literate in Shilghati Village, Udaipur, Tripura

	Total No. of Households	*No. of literatre people*	*Matriculates and (10+2) stage*	*B.A.*	*M.A.*	*Engineers*	*Doctors*
Men	720	525	40	15	2	5	2
Women	780	475	25	7	1	—	—
Total	1500	1000	65	22	3	5	2

Sources: (a) Sri Gandha Chandra Jamatia, Chakdiri, Shilghati village, Udaipur, Tripura.

(b) Sri Rajendra Jamatia, a teacher of a school who is entrusted by Jamatia Hoda to collect data regarding education of the village Shighati.

From the above table it is found that out of 780 women, 25, 7 and 1 are Matriculates and Plus Two Passed, graduates and Post graduate respectively. There are no female engineer, doctor, and other Prominent post holders.

The Religious Status

As the Jamatia women are not permitted socially to become Akra, Panchays, or Chakdiris, so in the same way the status of a woman in the matter of religious rites is much lower than that of man. The women are prohibited from becoming an Ochay of their community. "The exclusion of Jamatia women from certain religious festivals and ritualistic observances like their periodical segregation during their periods appears not to be due to any assumed inferiority in their status but due to the tribals horror of menstrual blood which is supposed to attract evil spirits" (Dr. Suchinta Bhattacharjee).In this time of period, they are not allowed to enter into the kitchen to cook nor can they attend any social function. The same attitudes prevail in many higher societies also where the women in menstrual period are not allowed to do the same things particularly the religious rituals and cooking.

But in the new transitional modern period, the status of women is gradually upgrading as they are able to establish themselves in almost all fields. Three women, one is a student and other two are the Government service holders and good housewives also, are taken into consideration. Their conversations are given below.

Questionnaire A

1.	Name of the Village/ Panchayat/ Sub-Division	:	Khamar Bari Teliamura, Khowai
	District	:	West Tripura
2.	Name of the Informant	:	Jemi Jamatia
3.	Name of the Community	:	Jamatia, Tribe: Scheduled Tribe
4	Educational Qualification	:	Class X Standard
5.	Present/Previous Working Status	:	Student
6.	Marital Status	:	Unmarried

7. Social Activities, if any : Nil
8. Economic Status (Present) : Dependent
9. How many members of your family are literate : Five Members.
10. Elite Role:-
    (a) Club : ____
    (b) Library : ____
    (c) Other prominent Committees : ____

Questionnaire B

1. What is your idea about the empowerment of women?

Ans: Women must get power.

2. At what age did you start your study?

Ans: At the age of 8 or 9.

3. How far these empowerment and status are achieved by the Tribal women of Tripura?

Ans: Girls like me from villages are now much interested in study, so tribal girls are coming forward.

4. Why have you come to study at Agartala?

Ans: My father is poor and so to provide me with study after the Madhyamik Exam is quite tough for my family. Here to get both the free school and hostel facilities on S.T. ground, I applied for hostel and got the chance to stay here.

5. Would you like to study more?

Ans: Yes. I would like to study at least up to graduation to manage any job to maintain my own livelihood.

6. What is your father's profession ?

Ans: Cultivation.

7. **Do all the girls of your village like the same profession of your father go to school?**

Ans: No. Not all but those have any relative or friend want to study at the town.

8. **Is bride price practiced in your family ? What is your opinion about it?**

Ans: These systems are now almost non-existent as the boys in our community hardly agree for 'Jamaikhata' system. And the 'Bride Price' system is also becoming obsolete. But I do support them.

9. **How do you support the new entry of dowry system in your community?**

Ans: Not at all. It is a great burden to poor families.

10. **How would then combat against this social curse?**

Ans: If every girls stand against it armed with education, then I think it will go.

Questionnaire A

1.	Name of the Village/ Panchayat/Sub-Division	:	Agartala, Sadar, College Tilla, Tripura West
2.	Name of the Informant	:	Sanchita Jamatia
3.	Name of the Community	:	Jamatia, Tribe: Scheduled Tribe
4	Educational Qualification	:	10+2
5.	Present/Previous Working Status	:	Government Service.
6.	Marital Status	:	Married
7.	Social Activities, if any	:	Nil
8.	Economic Status (Present)	:	Independent
9.	How many members of your family are literate	:	Four Members
10.	Elite Role:-		
	(a) Club	:	——

(b) Library : ____

(c) Other prominent Committees : ____

Questionnaire B

1. **What is your idea about the empowerment of women?**

Ans: Women's power to do everything freely and fairly.

2. **Do you feel that empowerment of women helps to achieve their desired status?**

Ans: Yes.

3. **How far these empowerment and status are achieved by the Tribal women of Tripura?**

Ans: Not so far.

4. **What plans and programmes do you think may be adopted by both the Central as well as the State Government to develop the status and Empowerment for the Tribal women of Tripura?**

Ans: To introduce more quotas for tribal women specially for the economically poor.

5. **Is there any distinction of treatment towards a boy child and a girl child in the Tribal society of Tripura?**

Ans: No.

6. **Did you ever face insecurity, suppression or any gender harassment in your working place ?**

Ans: No.

7. **Is bride price practiced in your family?**

Ans: Now a days no one is getting any interest in this practice.

8. **The dowry is also entering in your community. Would you support it?**

Ans: No.

9. Do you ever felt any guilt for not giving enough time or care to your family?

Ans: I meet equally to my both ends.

10. Any message for the new generation tribal from your side?

Ans: To get oneself educated and acquire economic independence.

Questionnaire A

1.	Name of the Town	:	Agartala
	District	:	West Tripura
2.	Name of the Informant	:	ANINDITA JAMATIA
3.	Name of the Community	:	Jamatia, Tribe: S.T.
4.	Educational Qualification	:	B.E. in Electrical Engineering
5.	Present/Previous Working Status	:	As Lecturer in T.E.C.
6.	Marital Status	:	Married
7.	Social Activities, if any	:	Nil
8.	Economic Status (Present)	:	Solvent and Independent Middle Class
9.	How many members of your family are literate	:	All
10.	Elite Role:-		
	(a) Club	:	____
	(b) Library	:	____
	(c) Other prominent Committees	:	____

Questionnaire B

1. What is your idea about the empowerment of women?

Ans. Empowerment of women means to create such an environment that women can be able to participate spontaneously and lead in all sphere of life like education, health, industrial development, law, administration etc. to make a prosperous country according to their ability.

2. **Do you feel that empowerment of women helps to achieve their desired status?**

Ans: Obviously because it will make them self confident.

3. **How far these empowerment and status are achieved by the Tribal women of Tripura?**

Ans: A few percentages of tribal women are doing Government Jobs and very few of them are holding good post. But it is found that their number is increasing day by day which is really a good sign.

4. **What plans and programmes do you think may be adopted by both the Central as well as the State Government to develop the status and Empowerment for the Tribal women of Tripura?**

Ans: There are various programmes taken by the Government for development of women and child, but it should be taken in care that the fund is utilized properly and the programmes are carried faithfully.

5. **Is there any distinction of treatment towards a boy child and a girl child in the Tribal society of Tripura?**

Ans: As far I know, in educated family it is not seen, but in a poor family when there comes a question of choice to give facility to any one child between girl child and boy, it is often for a boy.

6. **Did you feel any discrimination while you pursue higher studies from your family or community?**

Ans: No. I never felt such discrimination. My parent nourished me and my sister who is also studying in IIT, Kharagpur with same care as well as my brother.

7. **What do you think the actual purpose of pursuing higher study for Tribal women should be - to manage a good career or to manage a high profiled husband or to do beneficial works for own community?**

Ans: To do all beneficial works for own community. Why is it for "own Community", not for the all?

8. **Women face insecurity, suppression, gender harassment in almost all male oriented places. What is your opinion and suggestions?**

Ans: I agree with this. For this I think it will be better if a cell or committee can be formed in all offices and organizations which will look after these problems and to take proper steps to stop this.

9. **In what ways the much forwarded and well established Tribal women can contribute for the well being and prosperity of mass Tribal women of Tripura?**

Ans: Well established tribal women can spend a part of their time and their salary for the education not only literal, also moral of other tribal women, because in childhood, a child is greatly impressed by mother, so to educate an woman means to educate the family.

10. **Any message for the new generation tribal from your side?**

Ans: Don't forget your root. It is often seen that when one becomes well established he/she just forget what he/she was and becomes self centred. But I think then your responsibility starts to uphold another one and give him all the facilities for which you had to struggle.

The Chakma Women

The Social Status

The Chakma Community of Tripura is divided into eight sents or clans and they are concentrated mostly in Kailasahar, Amarpur and Sabroom sub-division. In numerical strength, the Chakmas are the fourth in position. Basically the social system of the Chakmas is patriarchal and as a result of it, in some spheres, specially in the sphere of female rights, the outlook to some extent was conservative. Previously the Jhum cultivation was the main source of economy in their life but now as they are opting for agriculture through plough cultivation on a permanent basis, a social change has hit them in the wave of their new life. With the spread of education, the Chakmas are taking various professions like services or trades. In rural areas, the Chakma women are supposed to do all household work like cooking, child rearing, weaving etc. though they are not very excellent in bamboo and cane work. On field work, they also help their men relating to all agricultural works. Besides housekeeping, they also engage themselves in marketing their household products. In urban areas, the literacy rate in the Chakma women is quite high and so a good number of Chakma women are educationally much forward than the Chakma men. In the percentage of holding good services in Government Department, the Chakma women outnumber their menfolk. Nowadays, almost all areas, both rural and urban, women education is much valued and is considered an essential asset for the girls. Naturally, the present day Chakma girls are attending schools and colleges and even to universities in large number. So though the social status of a Chakma woman is not equal to with their men, the coming days will gradually diminish the gap to treat them equal in their family and society.

The Marital Status

Two types of marriages are prevalent in the Chakma society. As a large number of Chakmas are Buddhists, the marriage performed by the Buddhist Bhiksus in accordance with the religious tenet is observed mostly by the advanced educated section of the people. Other one is the traditional one performed by the village ojhas. In both cases, child marriage is not permitted though rarely, it is seen in some cases. The usual practice of 'bride-price' or trial marriage like 'Jamaikhata' in the Tribal society of Tripura are not so rigidly practiced in the Chakma society. They follow their age old social custom in their marriage system. The Chakma man can follow polygamy as he is permitted socially to do it. Though modern educated men opted to enter into wedlock only once, men with more than one wives are rare which denotes the lower marital status of women definitely. Moreover the Chakma women cannot inherit their father's property as the sons are the only legal heir. In absence of any son, only then the daughters will be the heir of the property. The widow cannot get the share of the property of her dead husband but if she does not marry again, in that case she will get a little share of the property to maintain herself. And if the dead man is issueless, his widow then only get the full property. Divorce is granted to both male and female on equal grounds. If divorce occurs willingly initiated from the husbands' side without any proper reason, then the husband has to give back all dowry, ornaments and everything he received in wedding to his separated wife. In such case, the husband is to give alimony to the wife upon her remarriage. In the Chakma society, mostly marriages and divorces are settled by their own customary laws so the exact amount of alimony or any fixed maintenance according to the husband's economic status is determined but the educated and economically well settled Chakma women can easily settle their divorce alimony according to the Judicial law of the Indian Constitution.

The Economic Status

The economic life of the Chakma women is revolving round cultivation and presently through only twenty to twenty five per cent of the Chakma population of Tripura is still embracing jhum or plain land cultivation works. The Chakma women are exceptionally talented in weaving and so in spinning and weaving, they manage good market in handloom industry. In the Chakma traditional weaving craft, men are also needed to supply some help by making some tools to this craft but the principle works like preparing threads from cotton, colouring of threads, giving designs are done by both Chakma women and Chakma girls also.They weave their clothes in their home made looms. Though Chakma women usually don't prefer drinking themselves but they prepare liquors at homes from rice and root of a kind of local plant. But now a days specially after 1950-60, the rapid spread of education changes the economic life of Chakma women as they advanced immensely comparing to the other tribal women of Tripura. Almost everywhere Chakma women are accommodating themselves easily in various Deptt. of Government and non-government projects. Some of them are able to hold some reputed higher posts in government offices.

The Religious Status

The Chakma community professes Buddhism and have been Buddhist since long. But at the same time a great number of them also embrace Hindu type religious rituals and deities. But nowhere either in pursuing

Buddhism nor in professing Hinduism, women are permitted to conduct any religious programmes. In the temple of Lord Buddha, monks are all male members. The chiefs of these temples are mostly old men who read holy books like the Tripitaks and at Agartara in many auspicious Buddhist festivals the same scene can be seen. So in following both the Buddhistic Tantras and the rituals of Hinduism, the head priest or the chief religious persons are always seleted from men and under their guidance the women only work as suppliers like sweeping and swabbing the temple's floors and stairs, mopping walls and cleaning utensils, collecting flowers and waters etc. In birth or death rituals, women have no entry through main road but just mere passive observers on every religious performance. Thus the religious status of the Chakma women is far below than their male counterparts. Of course the Chakma community keeps itself at a safe distance from the Christianity.

In the case of Chakma women also, three sample surveys have been done, three women, one is a student and other two are the much noted ladies, one is holding of Joint Director of Higher Education of Tripura Government and the second one is the Superintendent of Physical Education, Government of Tripura. Their views are recorded here as it has been told by them.

Questionnaire 'A'

1.	Name of the Village/ Block/Panchayat	:	Tilakpara
	Sub-Division	:	Gandachara, Dhalai
2.	Name of the Informant	:	Monsoon Chakma
3.	Name of the Community	:	Chakma, Tribe: S.T.
4.	Educational Qualification	:	Class XI
5.	Present/Previous Working Status	:	Student
6.	Marital Status	:	Unmarried

7.	Social Activities, if any	:	Nil
8.	Economic Status (Present)	:	Dependent
9.	How many members of your family are literate	:	Four including parents
10.	Any social activities	:	No, not yet.

Questionnaire 'B'

1. **At what age did you start your study ?**

Ans: At 6 +

2. **What is the profession of your father ?**

Ans: Service.

2. **What is your idea about the empowerment of women ?**

Ans: Women's power to judge and to decide everything of their likings.

3. **How far this empowerment is achieved by the Tribal women of Tripura?**

Ans: A little bit.

4. **Would you like to study more ?**

Ans: My ambition is to continue my study up to Master Degree level. Now college and university education, both are essential for acquiring a good job. So I will try to take the higher education.

5. **Do all the girls of your village go to school ?**

Ans: Almost 100 percent. Now in every accessible distance, there is at least one balwadi school or Junior basic school and the awareness of the girls education is also spreading among the villagers. So almost everyone sends their girls to schools.

6. **Is 'Bride Price' practiced in your family ? Do you support it?**

Ans: No, And though it is not practiced in our community, I think it is not so bad, at least for the poor family.

7. Then do you support the dowry system that is invading your community?

Ans: No. It should not be allowed to enter our community.

8. How would you fight against this curse?

Ans: We should be careful not to copy other's negative side.

9. What do you think the actual purpose of pursuing higher study for tribal women to manage a good career or to manage a high profiled husband or to do beneficial works for own community?

Ans: First to establish a career, otherwise other two attempts would not be possible.

10. How would you like to serve your community?

Ans: I would serve for women of any community.

Our second Chakma woman is Smt. Manika Talukder who started her career as a teacher, then the Assistant Headmistress of the H.S. School and then the Headmistress and finally as Deputy Director and Joint Director of the Higher Education of Tripura Government.

Questionnaire A

1.	Name of the Town/ Municipality/Block/Ward No./Subdivision	:	Agartala, Melarmath, 7th (Agartala), Rabindra Palli.
2.	Name of the Informant	:	Smt. Manika Talukder
3.	Name of the Community	:	Chakma Tribe: S.T.
4.	Education Qualification	:	M.A. B.Ed.
5.	Present/Previous Working Status	:	Joint Director of Higher Education/Headmistress of H.S. School.

6.	Marital Status	:	Divorcee
7.	Social Activities, if any	:	Yes
8.	Economic Status (Present)	:	Gazetteer Govt. Service
9.	How many members of your family are literate	:	One member family So one
10.	Elite Role:-		
	(a) Club	:	At present-No, for ill health
	(b) Library	:	Yes
	(c) Other prominent Committees	:	At present-No, for ill health

Questionnaire B

1. **When did you first start your study ?**

Ans: I started my education first at 4+ and passed H.S. also at 16+

2. **What was the condition of girls particularly the tribal girls who wanted to study at that time ?**

Ans: There was little school education but college education was also almost nil for the tribal girls at our time.

3. **Did you get the full opportunity to study the level you wanted from your family?**

Ans: Yes. In my case I got full opportunity to pursue higher study.

4. **Did you feel any discriminatory attitude or treatment from your family or from your community for being a girl?**

Ans: Equal treatment has been given to me from my family but from community my higher study was not liked so much.

5. **What was your purpose to pursue higher study to get a good career or to get a high profiled husband?**

Ans: To stand on my own feet with dignity, self independence was must and that was my primary aim to pursue higher study.

6. **Did you feel any egocentric problem or conflict in your conjugal settlement for your individual achievement ?**

Ans: There was no egocentric problem specially in our professional fields. No interference was made on anyone's individual area from both sides.

7. **Women mostly face insecurity, suppression, gender harassment in male dominated working place. Did you ever face such problem?**

Ans: Being a women holding higher post, I had to face such problems both in my working place and also in my joint in law's family. Lastly I overcome every problems with my weapons-education and good economic status. And in my working places, after doing long struggle with the indiscriminate attitude of the male dominated world, I have succeeded everything with my mental strength. Now I am quite happy both in my working place and at my home also.

8. **For your busy outside schedule, did you ever feel any guilt for not giving enough time towards your family?**

Ans: I have done my best and so no question of guilt arises.

9. **Do you find any difference at your time and now in pursuing higher study of the Tribal girls?**

Ans: Schooling was then the certificate for marriage but now every tribal girls from nook and corner, are reaching to colleges and university. Even parents of village background don't feel land property enough security, they even prefer self independent groom for their daughters. And now girls are much more conscious of these things.

10. **Any message from your side for the tribal women of the present generation?**

Ans: (a) I think the tribal girls should possess more seriousness and sincerity in pursuing education specially higher study and also develop the quality of personal life, professional career and family life.

(b) They must develop their mental status means self dignity and consciousness of one's own value.

(c) Regarding moral value pains today's society. So moral, ethical and humane sense with proper discipline are must for today's women.

(d) Tribal girls should develop confidence in themselves.

(e) They should maintain their own cultural heritage and language properly. Higher education must not make them artificial and forgetful to their cultural root.

1.	Name of the Town	:	Sabroom
	District	:	South Tripura
2.	Name of the Informant	:	Juthika Chakma
3.	Name of the Community	:	Chakma, Tribe: Tribal of Tripura
4.	Educational Qualification	:	B.A., M.P.E.D.
5.	Present/Previous Working Status	:	Supdt, Physical Education
6.	Marital Status	:	Married
7.	Social Activities, if any	:	No
8.	Economic Status (Present)	:	Group B (Gazetted)
9.	How many members of your family are literate	:	Two

10. Elite Role:-
 (a) Club : ____
 (b) Library : ____
 (c) Other prominent Committees : ____

Questionnaire B

1. **What is your idea about the empowerment of women?**

Ans. Empowerment of women will be beneficial and helpful to other Tribal women in developing foresightness.

2. **Do you feel that empowerment of women helps to achieve their desired status?**

Ans: Being friendly and maintaining social status, Tribal women enable themselves to come out successful in this field.

3. **How far these empowerment and status are achieved by the Tribal women of Tripura?**

Ans: Neighbours are also consulted if needed, may be educated and advised for proper guidance in respect of prevalent facilities and awareness.

4. **What plans and programmes do you think may be adopted by both the Central as well as the State Government to develop the status and Empowerment for the Tribal women of Tripura?**

Ans: Facilities of schools in villages, free education and books up to class X standard, free coaching,granting of scholarship for the meritorious pupils.

5. **Is there any distinction of treatment towards a boy child and a girl child in the Tribal society of Tripura?**

Ans: There is hardly any distinction between male and female babies.

6. **Did you feel any discrimination while you pursue higher studies from your family or community?**

Ans: No, Tribal women little feel any discrimination.

7. **What do you think the actual purpose of pursuing higher study for Tribal women should be - to manage a good career or to manage a high profiled husband or to do beneficial works for own community?**

Ans: Of course, Tribal women pursue higher study to make good career.

8. **Women face insecurity,suppression,gender harassment in almost all male oriented places. What is your opinion and suggestions?**

Ans: Tribal women little face gender harassment but in case of security and suppression they should group and lodge complaint with the village elders/Gram Pradhans etc.

9. **In what ways the much forwarded and well established Tribal women can contribute for the well being and prosperity of mass Tribal women of Tripura?**

Ans: Tribal women can be guided in developing in the Arts, handicrafts, weaving, sewing, knitting etc.

10. **Any message for the new generation tribal from your side?**

Ans: New generations may also be educated in the fields of Arts and culture, sports, music apart from essential educational qualifications.

Thus from the opinions of these girls of four different S.T. communities who are now students of class X to

University level, and some well established elderly women quite renowned on their own qualities, it is proved that the tribal women are no more in their slumber as they are marching forward with clear consciousness of acquiring good quality of education, economic standard and well established jobs. The girls who are students of school, do not want to discontinue their studies after school level only. Most of them are now aspiring for both college and university degrees to grab a good independent position of their own from where they can dictate and demand the things of their choice. At the same time, all these women are well conscious to retain their own tribal culture and traditional spirit along with their higher standard of life which are healthy expressions of good education. The most remarkable thing is that even the poor village parents send their girls far from their village to town to get the facilities of good education and this awareness is reaching at every remote and far flung areas. The awareness for girl's education becomes much active particularly within the few years of the last decade. As the census report of 2001 regarding S.T. literacy rate is yet to be published, let us have a look of the early five years of the last decade. The Five Years Achievements of Tribal Welfare Department, 1993-94 to 1997-98, Government of Tripura reports this way.

According to 1991 census, total population of Tripura is 27,57,205 out of which tribal population is 8, 53, 345 which accounts for 30.95 per cent of the total population. The literacy rate among the tribal women is still very low and it is only 27.34 per cent. The drop out rates at primary level in T.S.P area is 74 per cent against 59 per cent of the state. Therefore the tribals in the state are culturally backward, economically underdeveloped and technically uncivilized. In order to bring these communities in terms with the growing changes and developments, the State

Government has undertaken many developmental programmes for their educational and economic development through implementation of various tribal welfare schemes in the state.

The state has adopted the Maharasthrian model of T.S.P in the year 1995-96. According to this, all the developed departments are to qualify 31 per cent of their plan funds earmarked as Tribal Sub Plan and book against the Budget Demand of Tribal Welfare Department. Various types of factors such as area, terrain, tribal culture, needs and aspirations of these tribal communities have to be taken into confidence before drawing up development plan.

1. Economic Development
2. Social Development
3. Infrastructure Development
4. Protective and Anti Exploitative Measures
   (a) Land Alienation
   (b) Reservations

In order to protect the interest of the tribals in employment, the Government has been implementing the policy of reservation strictly. In this respect we can mention the report that National S.C. and S.T. commission requested the Government of Tripura to strictly implement the laws on fake S.T./S.C. certificate holders according to the article 5th of 338 of the Indian Constitution. (*Source*: PIB, New Delhi, 10th January 2002). Comprehensive law has been enacted by the Government namely, The Tripura S.C. /S.T. (Reservation of Vacancies in Services and Post) Act 1991 to prevent violation of the principle of reservation in services.

   (c) Forest Policy
   (d) Excise Policy

5. Institutional Framework for welfare of S.T.

In order to strengthen the efforts of Tribal Welfare Department, the other relevant institutions are the T T A A D C, Tribal Research Institute, T.R.P., P.G.P. and S.T. Development Corporation.

Moreover, for the rapid development of the girls education, fifty per cent of the total number of stipends is reserved for students belonging to S.T./S.C. and O.B.C. classes. Out of the remaining 50 per cent, one third is reserved for girl students. Special stipends have been instituted for girl students undergoing higher education.

At the post Metric stage also, they are given special stipends from the government of India funds. The Examination fees paid by S.T. and S.C. students of Schools and colleges are reimbursed by the state government, while tribal financial Assistance is also given to deserving students for purchasing of books.

The other beneficial works for the girls are also undertaken and according to the planning, works on different fields has already been started. In order to provide basic educational facilities to inaccessible tribal areas, girls hostels are being constructed under the centrally sponsored scheme on 50:50 basis. During the period from 1993-94 to 1997-98,an amount of Rs. 210-74 lakh was utilized for construction of girls hostels. Let us see the picture clearly...

Completed Hostels For Girls

1. Surendra Nagar	30 seated
2. Ratanpur	40 seated
3. Laxmicherra	30 seated
4. Teliabari	25 seated
5. Jatanbari	50 seated
6. Manughat	50 seated
7. Damchara	50 seated
8. Ananda Bazar	50 seated

9. Durgaram	50	seated
10. Kanchanpur	50	seated
11. Palace Compound	100	seated

On going Construction

1. Colonel Choumuhuni	50	seated
2. Amarpur	30	seated
3. Khowai Government Girls	50	seated
4. Jampai Jala	20	seated
5. Sabroom Government Girls	50	seated
6. Chawmanu	100	seated
7. Chailengta	50	seated

Almost all the developing programmes undertaken as given above are completed or on the way of completion. All these development works should reach to the grass root level where the poorest people of all the remotest corners get real benefit of these programmes.

It is also noticed that despite many government programmes and works done for the benefits of the tribal people of Tripura, the total progress of education particularly at the rural level and remote places is yet not satisfactory. Previously poor communication system was held responsible for it. But now the general communication system is not in the primitive stage any more. The number of Government Schools and Government Aided schools in Tripura is the highest in comparison with any other states of India. Besides these schools, the private schools also there whose numbers are also not very few. The literacy rate in Tripura as a whole is also very encouraging.

The actual fact is that much before and after the formation of Bangladesh in 1970, many uprooted Bengali took shelter in Tripura who were culturally and educationally already more developed than the hill people and so after their new settlement in Tripura and particularly after Tripura's accession to Indian Territory, education started normally in them and in this way the percentage of literacy in Tripura actually surpassed not only the North East States but also became much better than many states of India. Once again let us tally the percentage of literacy of Tripura with India at a glance.

Literacy Rate and the Number of Schools at a Glance

1. Literacy rate at the state	60.44 %
2. Literacy rate in men	70.58 %
3. Literacy rate in women	49.65 %
4. The number of Primary Schools	2081
5. The number of Middle Schools	424
6. The number of Madhyamik	407
7. The number of H.S. School	224
8. The number of of Primary Schools Under A.D.C.	1273

Literacy Rate (1991 Census)

Total literacy rate	60.44 % (52.21% in India)
Men	70.58 % (68.23% in India)
Women	49.65 % (39.29% in India)
Rural	56.08 %
Urbal	83.09 %
Total literacy rate of S.T.	40.37 % (19.60% in India)
Men	52.88 % (40.65% in India)
Women	27.34 per cent (18.19% in India)

Admission of Girls and Boys at Primary level (from Class I to V

	1997-98	*2000-2001*	
Total	4,40,886	4,69,562	(89.70%)
Boys	2,39,958	2,48,325	(97.70%
Girls	2,00,928	2,21,237	(81.20%)
Total S.T.	1,46,380	1,65,705	(90.73%)

From VI to VIII

	1997-98	*2000-01*	
Total	60,410	1,53,907	(58.40%)
Boys	35,159	82,880	(66.40%)
Girls	25,251	71,027	(40.50%)
Total S.T.	13,048	40,151	(43.29%)

From IX to X (2000—2001)

Total	71,047	(40.42%)
Boys	38,972	(43.53%)
Girls	32075	(37.18%)
Total S.T.	17,859	(32.83%)

From XI to XII

Total	25,555	(15.56%)
Boys	16,411	(18.94%)
Girls	10,144	(12.06%)
Total S.T.	2,890	(5.47%)

Total Girls School (2000-2001)

Middle	8
Madhyamik	25
H.S.	23

Comparative Picture of drop outs in Tripura and India (From class I to X)

	Tripura	*India*
Total	80.17%	69.42%
Boys	79.67%	66.82%
Girls	80.75%	73.04%
S.T.	88.14%	—

Source : Tripura Darpan, Tathyapangi 0 Nirdeshika 2001.

The facts which are provided in the foregoing pages, it is quite evident that Tripura though industrially, geographically and economically backward, is much forward educationally at least in considering the literacy rate and the number of schools both government and government aided and also non-government in such a tiny state. At the same time, the number of girl students are not much less than the boys and besides the co-education schools where the same number of boys and girls can study, the schools only for girls are outnumbering also, from class I to X, the gap of the percentage in attendance between the boys and the girls is quite insignificant. Only in H.S. level, that is in class XI and XII, the average presence of the S.T. students is quite less. This is because after the Madhyamik level, the S.T. students of needy background engage in different posts reserved for them. Only a small percentage opt for graduation and then post graduation because much before that, they get employed in different levels with H.S. pass certificate.

The picture of dropouts in Tripura is something thought provoking. The level of drop outs is much higher both in general and backward students equally which is much higher than the national level. This again proves that negative infrastructure of poor economy, communication and lack of desire to provide requisite time to acquire a minimum degree for completion of a full course of study of the general and particularly of the hill people.

So the literacy among the tribals particularly in tribal women is still not at all satisfactory. The so called language problem which poses acute problem to the tribals as they have to follow their classes and take exams in languages other than their mother tongues. The teachers who impart them lessons and lectures are not of their tribal origin. So both the lessons and the lesson givers may appear dull which may fail to create acute interest in them.

Though this picture is very true but to fight this problem is a long time consuming process and not easy at all. All the kings of Tripura used to do all sorts of their works in Bengali and from then, Bengali language got the official status in Tripura, but the common, poor and ignorant hill people converse in their dialects. This old picture is somewhat the same still today. The tribal students of urban area do much better than students of rural schools in academic life in spite of this language bar. And as tribals still today are mostly settled in rural areas, special attention with careful planning should be taken to bring a fruitful result.

To combat the problem at the first level, the linguistic policy of Tripura should be considered first and foremost. All the nineteen tribes of Tripura cannot speak in Kokbarak and the hurdle is not finished here. The Kokbarak language is also not comprehensively developed and still it is in the developing stage. So as long as any clear cut linguistic policy is not formulated, developed and enriched, the tribals of Tripura have to follow their education at least up to secondary level in Bengali. Besides, the use of Bengali in books, availability of trained teachers, library etc. are also needed. The problem is more acute in rural areas because facilities and economic condition are more there. The rural students are used to devote less time to their study either for less awareness, less competitiveness or for less time as they earn money for their families.

Though this language problems is acute, all other areas regarding the development of women education, status and empowerment are not quite up to the mark. The 33 per cent of women Reservation Bill in State Legislatures and Lok Sabha is still in its mother's womb and almost one and half decades have passed just for placement of the Bill in the parliament. The Parliament sessions without number passed just in fighting on the issue whether the Bill should be passed or not. It gives the clear picture of India that Parliament is still a male bastion which is a hard nut to crack. The few microscopic female members fail to cope up with their male members to give the Bill its final birth. Let's hope the day is not too far when the Bill will be passed finally to give women their long dues.

Women in the Garo, the Kuki, the Mug, the Lushai and the Halam community

Other than these four major tribes, the women of remaining fifteen tribes namely the Halam, the Noatia, the Mog, the Kuki, the Uchai, the Khasi, the Bhil, the Lepcha, the Bhutia and the Chaimal are still today mostly reside on isolated areas of hills and remote corners of Tripura. It is a fact that centuries of social repression have installed in the mind of tribals a feeling of insecurity and it is not surprising that they suffer quite naturally an inferior complexity. Actually next to Africa, India has the largest concentration of tribal population and though a lot has been done for their social and economical betterment, yet a major portion of their population remains in the dark to avail themselves of the opportunities. Further, more development amongst the tribes themselves is not uniform. The tribals of urban areas of Tripura have attained much forward status due to influence of acculturation of plain people. But still except the four major tribes as discussed on the aforesaid pages, the other tribal people's development exhibit varying stages of slow and low progress as they are still living outside the sphere of influence of modern civilization, isolated in hills and forests and living by primitive method of cultivation and food gathering.

Quite naturally, there are a little number of studies of these above mentioned fifteen tribes on their culture, dress, food, drink, and the socio cultural problems but these issues have not been properly focused in relation to their women. The study of these tribal women become important because the problems of them differ from a particular area to another area owing to their geographical locations, historical background and the processes of social change.

Though most of the writers, researchers and scholars like Hutton(1921), Furer-hai mendorf(1943), Hunter(1973), & Firth(1946) reported the higher social status of women, there are some pit holes which cannot be denied also. The popular image & perception of the tribal women is that they enjoy much better social status than their non tribal counterparts as the Tribal Women have no fear of early marriage, no stigma of widow hood, have the freedom of divorce and remarriage and earns in her own way to get economic independence. But her low status is equally important as she does not have property rights except in a matrilineal society which is a small proportion of the tribal population. She is less paid on equal work than her male counterparts. She cannot hold the office of a priest, neither is allowed to touch the plough { now a days plain land cultivation is fast becoming their alternative} or participate in the roofing of a house. women of some tribal groups cannot be allowed to enter in to the temple or attend any communal worship. Thus the status of tribal women sometimes varies from tribe to tribe a little bit. Therefore, the social status of the Tribal Women of Tripura is little bit peculiar compared to their non tribal sisters. The prevalence of bride price as contrasted to dowry, the existence of matrilineal and matriarchal society mostly sometimes confirm the higher social status of the tribal women . But in Tribal society also, there are clearly defined areas of work among the males and the females. Along with men folk in economic activities and earning livelihood, tribal women participate in all agricultural operations except ploughing. The division of work is heavily loaded against the tribal women because in addition to an equal share in the production of economy, she also bears the burden of all house hold works. A tribal woman carries both the loads on her head along with her child on her back which is unthinkable for a working tribal man . So traditionally, on working load, the tribal woman is enormously handicapped. Being a women she is already handicapped as all women are in matter of education & economy independence, she is doubly handicapped for belong to a disadvantaged section of tribal society. The importance of the tribal women in their society is significant because of the fact that the tribal women work harder almost relentlessly and the family economy and management depend on them. The Tribal woman of the house has to work in the family as a wife, a mother and an earner which corroborates in traditional societies with a primitive economy where her role is that of a 'breeder, feeder and producer' of goods. Her income of both in cash and kind is considered as household income and the income in kind is sold in the market to transform it in cash which is kept by her husband as he usually goes to the market. The unrecognized role of a silent worker is primarily because the tribal women are not empowered to take decisions both inside & outside of her family which remains the prerogative of the males of the family. The tribal women thus remain to be deprived to despite performing various ascribed roles as their employment and income earning potential go unrecognized. At the cost of their own health, they take care and contribute to the health of their families.

Under the above discussion, let us find out the role and the status of women starting from the Garo community. The actual fact is that, except the Tripuris which is also an admixture of different clans and sub clans, the other eight tribes mentioned in the Government gazette are immigrants tribes to Tripura. The Garo is one of them.

The Garo

The Social Status:- The position of women in a Garo society shatters the myth of the higher status of women in a matriarchal & matrilineal society. The social position of the Garo women has not been favourarbly affected by their matriarchal system. The social life of the Garo women is very well knit and disciplined as they allowed their husband plays a prominent role as the head of the family for all purposes. The question of absolute supremacy of women does not arise so far as men are neither dominated nor ill treated or suppressed . On the contrary the Garo husband folk receive respect from women folk and command immense authority in their household establishment after marrying Garo women. Therefore the social status of the Garo women is obviously little equal if not low as they are treated only as a vehicle by which property descends from one generation to another.

For the Garos, 'Custom' is the law of the land which is observed from time immemorial. Customary law has its originality antiquity, certainly, continuity and it has the force of law governing the whole Garo tribe. The Garo society that pin so much importance and value to matriarchal does not pay absolute authority and social status to its women. The decline in the vitality of the Jhum economy, growing dependence on non traditional sources of income, etc are strengthening this mentality with the recent steady decline in sex position of the Garo women.

The Marital status: Though the marriage proposal comes from women, but it is settled and materialized by the male relatives without the permission of the male members of family, a Garo widow can never claim a re marriage and she may be forced to marry for sole consideration of property. But a man can easily marry for second time along with his first wife by just manage to influence his first wife for her consent.

The powerful women who are notionally owners of land and property are known as mahari. Yet the husband of a mahari is less authoritative than his wife as he is always looked upon as the owner of the lands of his wife for his wife is the source of his power which he derives through his wife's free hand to let him exercise. In a Garo Society, a man can marry the widow of his uncle but in case this widow aunti refuses to marry her husband's nephew, the nephew may claim compensation. The law of inheritance is matrilineal & it goes to the best daughter of the family. She is known as Nokna & her husband is known as Nokkrom who after marriage must reside at his father in law's house and has no right of his wife's ancestral property . So like patriarchal society, the maintenance to the female member does not arise. But as long as father is alive, it is obligatory for him to maintain his wife, minor children, unmarried daughter, his widower Nokkrom and widow Nokna daughter till a substitute is provided by the clan members. If the father dies, the question of mother's responsibility arises but if she marries again, the responsibility goes to step father but if the mother remarries outside the clan, she loses the right of her ancestral property. In her place, one of the daughters takes the responsibility.

Divorce is granted on mutual consent but for the fault of one partner, the compensation or the maintenance which is called 'dai' must be provided by the party to be blamed. In case of desertion of a Garo woman by her husband, she can ask for another substitute husband instead of maintenance from her husband's clan. If she is not provided with this marriage the compulsion to marry from her husband's clan subsides and she is free to marry any one according to her living.

Thus the marital status of the Garo women is not as high as expected in a matrilineal society. It must be mentioned that lack of education is the main hindrance in securing the power, establishing the command, placing the decision though they are entitled for the property right.

The Economic Status: Economic development is a problem of women in general and the tribal women in particular. The problem becomes more surmountable of backward hilly regions inhabited by tribal people which reflects the co existence of many problems namely economic, geographical & sociological. The low level of literacy is the most acute problem for any progress of economic development. Even today, more than two third of the Garo population is illiterate. Literacy, education and subsequent good & sound economy have a great bearing on the status of women by enabling them to take right decision & earn a living. But the Garo women instead of their superior status of matrilineal society, fail to hold their grip on economic fields. Men being the head of the family and of the clan, exercise their full strength & authority on administrative & management. Women are rather 'passive', titular inheritors of property in name only. It is a fact that women take part in the clan and the family matters upon a large extent, the functions & powers do not come even near equal to that of the father who is actually the supreme authority of family's administration & economy.

In the economic management, where property passes on from the mother to the daughter, men folk have no important function except the father who has the right to decide the qualities of daughters to inherit the property as his own earned property also goes to this principal property. Here, the father is specially selective for someone close from his mother's family such as his own maternal nephew or grand nephew to inherit by marrying his inheriting daughter for keeping his own lineage in the property earned by his own uncle or grand uncles etc.

Jhum cultivation along with other vegetables is main source of economy of the Garos . The Garo women are the main supplier of their physical labour towards the field as well as domestic household works like brewing & weaving, husking rice& pressing oilseeds, collecting firewoods &fetching water, feeding pigs & poultry, carding cotton & spinning yearn, weaving cloth & cooking food and so on. The Garo women are specially skilled in weaving their own ethnic clothes and almost every house wife has rough loom.

So the strong matrilineal background does not save the women to contribute their unpaid & un rewarded work load to the welfare of their families at the cost of their effort, time and sincerity which could have fetch remuneration if done else where as job or as worker.

The Religious Status : Like other areas, religion and its practice undergone a change in the Garo's life also. It is an undisputed fact the Garos are more at home with God and events pertaining to the divine and super natural things. The words of J.H. Hutton must be mentioned here,.... "The beliefs held by the tribals are not imaginings of superstitions & untaught minds ... but the debris of a real religious system, a definite philosophy...."

The Garos believe in the existence of a supreme deity who is sometimes identified as Tatara Rabuga. All other lesser deities are also male like Saljong, Nosta- Nopantu, Chorabudi, Goera etc. Two or three female deities are there also like Susime, Asima- Dingsima etc. But whatever may be the God the priest hood is strictly maintained by male members. The Chief Priest is called Kamal and the office of the Kamal is not hereditary, nor is restricted to any particular class. The Women are only allowed to enter in to priesthood to perform some restricted religious duties. With the contributing facts of education, though religion is interwoven in every phase of a Garo's life, the primitive methods and practices likes sacrifices of animals are fast disappearing. The entry of Christianity is another factor to receding fast of their religious practices & beliefs. A correlation between Christianity, spread of literacy & modernization bring religious change, in a great measure yet the traditional old beliefs that is biased against women from performing any religious rituals with great authority and leading role. So like all other religions the status of the Garo women is much lower than their male counterpart as the religious field remains one of the male bastions still now. It is only at the time of delivery, the female kamal is called and at this time no male is allowed inside the delivery place. Apart from severing the naval chord, the Kamal also officiates at certain rituals restricting the birth ceremonies only.

The Garo women like their Hindu sisters performing Laxmi Puja have independent right to perform Pujas of Ronadik rites, the female Goddess of rice & wealth. Thus the Garo women have little right to perform religious rituals in case of little lower deities & goddess which clearly prove their lower religious status.

The Kuki

The exact origin of the kukis cannot be traced out after so long lapse of time & years but from different scholars and anthropologist's research, it is found that the original home of the Kuki is in the Chin Hills. Now they are found as neighbour of the Nagas in Assam and in contiguity with the Mugs of Arracan . They are divided into clans, each under its own chief, whose office was not hereditary but elective, but prefers a particular family or families for selection of such chief. The Kukis are nomadic by nature and have the habit of changing frequently their place of living by migrating from one state to another in search of fertile Jhum land & other reasons relating to it. This emigrating nature of the Kukis spread them towards the north eastern regions of India and Tripura is one of them.

Let us now throw light on the position of the Kuki women on social, matrimonial, economic and religious ground. As the literacy rate among the general Kukis is extremely low, the women in particular suffer this shortcoming for more than one reason. Since education is probably the most effective instrument for ensuring equality of opportunity, the Kuki women are lagging behind their more fortunate fellow sister of other tribal groups.

The Social Status: The population chart of previous decades 1971 of Tripura census shows that the female population of the Kukis was higher than the male population figuring 3,606 are males & 4169 are females with the span of thirty years, the female population has come down a little which, though not so much alarming like the difference of gender in general population, yet the trend is not healthy also. Though the Kukis are extremely indolent and the male members don't show any interest of works except barely necessary work, the whole load of work is left to their unfortunate women.

The males usually spend time in smoking, drinking and generally loafing. The women on the other hand bears the most hardship of life carrying every responsibility of works both inside the house as well as outside the field. Circumstances compels her to be extremely industrious as she gives her time in child rearing, house keeping, cooking, cleaning, cattle rearing, brewing and preparing cloths in her own looms. From dawn to dusk, she is on her toes to shift from one set of work to another tirelessly without any remuneration and sympathy. Naturally though her young days retain her natural beauty but her advanced days of hard life erodes her normal look very rapidly.

In spite of the fact that the Kuki women are supposed to the three forth of work load, yet their society generally welcomes a male child. They observe separate custom for their male child at its birth which definitely indicate their bias attitude towards gender discrimination Only in naming the first child, the mother gets the preferences to make a selection of name according to her likings. Though it is the most insignificant power to be mention worthy.

The Marital Status: Regarding marriage, the Kukis never marry outside their tribe, neither they observe any social customs. Usually, the women get married at early age and the bride is invariably purchased. In Suren Debarman's Jibon O Sanskriti', Hutchinson's Chittagong Hill tracts, Edward Tuite Dalton's Tribal History of Eastern India and also Ram Gopal singh's the Kukis of Tripura, observations regarding premarital sex of the Kukis are more or less the same. The Kuki women enjoy her freedom enormously in selecting her own spouse. Actually probationary marriage can be called as primitive version of modern practice of courtship before marriage. In this probationary period, the would be husband and wife are permitted to live together for sometime in the bride's house and their mutual consent leads this probation marriage into actual marriage. In case of disagreement between the couple, separation is easily allowed to them. Only a monetary penalty of cash compensation to the girl's parents is to be made from the boy's side. Thus premarital cohabitation, though an offence as long as it does not lead to pregnancy, is over looked, as most of the cases almost always ended in marriage.

Regarding the practice of premarital sex among the tribes, sometimes untoward situation arises due to the unnecessary controversies & forceful absurd denials brought by some of the so called educated tribals who with their adopted Christian religion and subsequently higher educational status with highest academic post, almost either forget or ashamed of admitting the real facts. It is extremely unhealthy to refuse one's own root as rootless trees die being uprooted totally. In our own modern language we call the premarital sex as trial marriage which is common not only in western countries but is starting to enter into our society though slowly but steadily. A miniscule number of modern & educated people even believe in 'live together' concept.

Like other tribals of Tripura, marriage by service which is a very common custom is not practiced by the Kukis. Only recently, after long staying side by side with other tribes of Tripura, the kukis of Tripura also some times indulge this practice . Monogamy rather than Polygamy is much prevalent in the Kukis. Widows are free to remarry anyone they like but within the one year of her previous husband's death she cannot marry. Only the chief who enjoys the highest social status, the widow or the widows of him cannot marry to retain the higher social status. Yet, if she marries, she is to abandon all her rank & status.

If a man deserts his wife without any reason, & no monetary compensation is being given by him, he has to leave single handedly. So widowhood or single status of a Kuki women is not a matter of concern as marriage custom is much more free. Of course, the present day situation is changing rapidly as civil court interferes to draw some monetary compensation in case of desertion. The biased attitude against women is found when after widowhood, she can marry only a widower & not a bachelor but a widower is free to marry anyone he likes.

Economic Status: Like all other tribes of Tripura, the Kukis also produce their crops through shifting of cultivation or Jhum. Though both men and women are engaged in the task of Jhum work, women bear most of the burden as they do all the household works besides the field work. Men never do the work specially allotted for women but women do most of the works generally done by men.

As literacy rate among tribal women in general and the Kuki women in particular is extremely low, they have been lagging behind all other section - urban males & females, rural male & family, S.C males & females, & tribal males, it is in the lowest rung in the Kuki women. Simultaneously the economic status also is low for them. Thus in spite of their heavy physical labour and the resultant hardship of it, the major portion of the benefit is reaped by the males. The impact of development programmes of both the central as well as the state governments has been different on different sections of tribal women. Mostly the urban based tribal women reap the full harvest of education and opportunities for employment. It is this section of advanced tribal women who enjoy economic benefits with self reliance, innovativeness and higher social & economic status to command an empowerment.

But the rural tribal women face new challenges as the Governmental control of forests adversely hit their agricultural economy. Besides agriculture, other work participation of the Kuki women is negligible. The Kuki society is patriarchal and therefore sons do inherit parental property. But the note worthy thing is that instead of the eldest son, the younger son succeeds to the largest share of property and parental house. The eldest son and other sons take shares from the remaining part. The eldest son gets little more than the other remaining sons. Economically, women of the Lushais Kukis of Tripura are today better advanced than the Darlong Kukis in matter of education and social advancement, though both the Kukis and the Lushais of Tripura are Jhumia, the extension of education through missionary activities, the orange economy of the Lushais in the Jampai Hill helped them to become more or less a stationary tribe.

The Religious Status: The Kukis are generally, according to Dr. Dwijendra Lal Bhowmik, in his Tribal Religion of Tripura 'Semi Hindus'. Though they were animistic wholly, but gradually they have adopted Hinduism . Since 1931, it is noted that some of the Kukis adopted Christian religion and since then the number of Christians have increased to a great extent though the number of Hindus among them is still greater.

But nowhere, whether it is Christian or Hindu Kuki women, she enjoys a complete authorative religious status. Even in tribal community where women constitute half or sometimes more than half population, their religious status is much lower than their male counterparts. She cannot hold the office of a priest and at the time of her menstruation she is not allowed to cross the area of worship like the non tribal communities. So at least in this point, the advanced and the primitive social communities treat their respective women in the same way.

The Mugs

In Rajmala, the story of the Mugs' entrance into Tripura has been stated that about 1380 years before, the King of Zugarufa defeated the King of Magada and won 'Rangamati', which is at present falls at Udaipur. He later placed his kingdom at Udaipur. From Hutchinson in his Chittagong Hill Tracts, we came to know that Mog is the popular designation of an Indo Chinese tribe who describe themselves by various titles of Maramagri, Bhuya magh, Jumiya magh and it is with the later who come from Burma.

Mugs are also known as Khyoungtha or children of the River who are of Arakanese origin, speak the ancient Arakan dialect and follow the Buddhist religion & customs. The Mugs are found along the banks of the chief rivers.

The Social Status: As still today in spite of the steady growth of education among the Mugs, both boys and girls of this community who are getting all the facilities of S.T group, may be considered the generation to taste the fruitfulness of education for the first time. Therefore the social condition of the Mugs is changing but very slowly. In Suren Debbarman's 'Jiban O Sankriti', it was written by Roybahadur Bipin Bihari Rakshit that the Mugs are unwilling to step outside the boundary of their own community and they are equally unaffected by other religion, culture, customs and mores and thereby were untouched from the light of education. Naturally, the status of women covering some important fields like social, marital, economical and religious more or less is the same with other S.T communities. Hutchinson in his Chittagong Hill Tracts paints the social life of the Mug women very accurately. "From marriage onwards, the life of the average Mug women is one of the constant toil and self denial and she will only find rest in death. In addition to her many and varied household cares and the duties and anxieties of maternity, she will have to work through all weathers in the field, sowing, weeding, harvesting, fetching and carrying for her indolent husband and devoting any spare time she may snatch to weaving clothes for home use. As she gets older and less comely, her duties become more arduous till, finally, at old age, she is systematically neglected and the rising generation take no trouble to conceal the fact that they consider her continued presence in the family circle a nuisance. The end comes at last and she is hurried away to the burning ghat where an extra couple of layers of wood are supplied to the funeral pyre in recognition of her position as the general provider for the family". The low social status of the Magh women is easily accountable and still today it has hardly changed.

Marital Status: The marital status of Mug women starts from the birth through un equal and biased rituals. On the birth of a son, guns are fired and a feast is given but not so when a daughter is born. Though 95% burden of domestic workload is on her shoulder,yet her position is sometimes like that of a slave. In Hutchinson's word " A chaste maiden life is a very rare exception........ but whatever her faults may have been as a maiden, when she married, chastity is a rule". Like the Hindus, the presence of a widow women in any marriage ceremony is forbidden. The custom of bride price is prevalent in the Mug society. A rich man can take more than one wife & in that case, the position of the first wife is much better. A widow or a deserted woman can marry again by her own choice and selection. The low marital status of Mug women can be cited by an important example of a newly married Mug girl as she was given to her husband by her father. "Take her"' the father says; "I have given her to you but she is young and not acquainted with her household duties. If therefore, at any time you come back from the Jhum and find the rice burnt, or anything else wrong, teach her - do not beat her but at the end of three years if she still continued ignorant, then beat her do not take her life- for if you do I shall demand the price of blood at your hands, but for beating her, I shall not hold you responsible or interfere". (Ref:The Hill Tracts of Chittagong by Captain Lewin -P-71). So wife beating is not a wrong practice at all. It seems that the the girl like an inanimate object is being shifted from one male hand to another male hand and if she is being killed by the husband only a price of monetary exchange is enough to wipe out this crime.

Economic Status: the Mugs are patriarchal society and in ordinary case the succession goes to the eldest son and where there are number of sons, one half will go to the eldest and one quarter to the youngest and the remaining quarter will go to the next sons. In case of two sons, the eldest will get the fifth eight and the three eight will go to the younger. But no property is given to the girls. Only where no male heir is available, the succession follows in the female line.

Most of the Mugs are Jumia but now a days they also cultivate in plain land though small in number. Like other tribal societies, most of the associate field works are done by women which are unpaid, unrecognized and unseen in addition to her everyday scheduled domestic work. Brewing is another field of work where women is supreme as they solely prepare it and the Mugs are highly liquor afflicted. Their Buddhist base don't refrain them from devouring liquor which religiously forbidden. Both men & women drink hugely but the preparation process lie in the hand of women solely without any remuneration. Tripura District Gazetters reports that the Mug women enjoy a great deal of freedom & they are very strong, stout & industrious. All household duties are performed by them & in leisure time, they weave their own garments.

Religious Status: The Mugs like the Chakmas are Buddhist. They consider it as their principal religion. They built temples of different size and employed the Buddhist priest who shaves his head and clothes himself with yellow garments. The villagers supply the cooked food for their priest. The males are entitled to get the priesthood as the young boys of the villages on attaining the age of eight or nine years are generally selected for the training of priesthood. For priesthood, these young boys go through some ceremonial rituals supported by their nearest male relatives of each. Women have no right to participate in this rite, but it is common for a man to perform it three to four times during his life.

The Mugs burn their dead. At the last journey, women get two layers of wood much from a man as the pyre is composed of five layers of wood for her, three for a man. Hutchinson called it a tribute for a woman for her lifetime service. Regarding the lighting of fire at the pyre, all nearest blood relatives of the deceased, both male or female have the right to fire the pyre. The dead bodies of rich people both male and female have the privilege to be carried to the burning ghat on a wheeled car. The funeral procession is led by the priests, then the male relatives and women come last.

The Halams

The Halams originally were one of the branches of the Kukis and it is said that they had lived in Tripura even before the Tripuris came in to conquer the land. From the very beginning, the Ttipuris established contacts with plain men, the Bengalis and benefited numerously establishing ruling territory up to the middle of 20th Century. At present, the Halams are also coming in contact with the plain people.

The Social status of the Halam women: The Halam tribe consists of some sub tribes namely Malsum, Kaipeng,

Rangkhal, Kalai, Rupiui and Bangcher. The social position of the women are almost the same of other tribal communities as women shoulder almost all the responsibilities of the house and field simultaneously. Family, connects of mostly three to four generation with married sons and daughters, unmarried members besides older parents. Free mixing and even talking with male members for a Halam wife specially with elder brother in law and maternal uncle in law is strictly restricted. Similarly, the brother in law and the maternal uncle in law can communicate if necessary through an intermediary with her. In her in laws place, she cannot move freely as she has to maintain some social restriction attributed to her.

The Marital Status: Widow marriage is in vogue with in the Halam community. The child marriage is rarely seen. But now days it is taking place in some areas. Marriage by service, by elopement, love marriage are common to the Halams but of all these marriage by service for the bride and by payment for the bride are most favourite types as the women are the economic backbone of the Halams. So long bargaining and discussions are needed to fix a bride price. The bride price consists of manual service by the prospective groom to the girl's house with the payment of both in cash and in kind. The boy's probation period of service to girls house lasts mostly three to four years. The economic loss as a result of her departure for good from her parents house made her parents to demand the bride price. The mother in law also get the same price or token as a price of her milk she feed to her daughter. In her primitive background, the Halam women's marital status is some what dignitary as she gets the bride price. She also divorces her first husband and seeks a second one in which case the children if any should go to the husband. In her new marital life, she is free from her old burden which definitely denotes a good position she enjoys. On the other hand no male can take a second wife in the life time of the first one unless a divorce is granted by the society. So both socially and martially the Halam woman enjoys a much better free position.

The Economic Status: The Economic life of the Halams centers round the hills and jungles to get the natural products in abundance. Besides the primitive agriculture of Jhum, the fishing, food gathering, weaving are in vogue with the Halam women. Weaving and brewing are two common fields totally controlled by them. Superstitious belief runs in to them that if the men set their hands in weaving, they face a bear's attack. Under the same belief women also refrain from preparing the work of basket making. So the economic position of the Halam women is quite sound as expected from a tribal society. Now a days the girls are attending schools and very few of them to colleges. But the awakening consciousness for girls education is now in the forefront in the Halam community to give their women a definite sound economic status.

The Halams are a patriarchal community. So generally the sons get all the property where as girls shift to their in laws house. In absence of any son only the daughter can get the share of her parental property.

The Religious Staus: It is reported by the Tripura District Gazetteers that the Halams are the follower of the 'Sakta' cult but the influence of vaishnavism is quite marked in two sections- Kalai and Rupini. They follow the form of worship as practiced by the Hindus and at the same time worship gods and goddesses in their own tribal way. At their puja place, no outsider is allowed to enter and the saying goes that the punishment for any tresspass is death. The women are debarred from doing any death rites of the decreased person. The priest is a male and it is the right of the first male in the line of succession to perform the rites. Only in the absence of any issue, the right goes to the wife. If there is no wife, then again the brother of the dead man can do the rite. So women have no direct authority to observe any religion rituals except when situation permits.

The Lushais

The Lushais are a powerful and independent people split up into different class. The District Tripura Gazetteers reports that the Lushai Kuki class were originally inhabitants of the hills lying to the east and north east of Tripura and to the adjoining hilly areas. In primitive times they were known as Kirats. The people of the Cachar call them Luchais. It is said that the word Lushais means head hunter. La means head and Chai means to cut. It is agreed that the word Lushai is the corrupted form of Luchai. The Lushais used to hunt heads at the time of the chieftains even as late as the middle of the 19th century which is now a matter of recorded past.

Although racially of the same origin, there is degree of difference between the Luchais and Kuki as far as culture and educational attainments are concerned. The spread of education through the Chriastian missionaries, the Lushais have advanced immensely embracing western dress and manners. Almost all of them have now turned to Christianity with rapid expansion of education in them and taking the benefits of Government efforts, the Lushais are now the enlightened community among the Tribal people of Tripura.

Sri Suren Deb Barman in his 'Tripurar Adibasi Jiban O Sanskriti' and Dr. Ramaprasad Dutta in his 'Tripura Lushai Kukider Itikatha' wrote that the Mizos are also a sub branch of the Lushais and they live in abundance in Tripura's Jampai Hill areas. Captain Lewin wrote " They differ entirely from the other hill tribes of Burman of Arracandes origin in that their faces bear no marks of Tatan or Mongolian descent. They are swarthy in complexion and their cheeks are generally smooth among the Howlong tribe. However, one meets many men having long busy beards. I should be inclined to attribute this to a mixture of Bengali blood ; for the many captives they have from time to time carried away".(Hill Tracts of Chittagong)

The Social Status: The Lushai women enjoy much more freedom than their male counterparts. They bear grave attitudes. Hunter in his A Statistical Account of Bengal wrote that the Lushai women are held in some sort of consideration, their advice is taken and they have much influence in their families. The wife becomes the head of the family upon the death of her husband. The whole burden of daily life, however falls upon the women who fetch water, collect dry leaves and wood, cultivate and help to reap the crops, besides spinning and cooking. The loin loom at which the women work in between their chores in the kitchen is usually placed in one corner of the kitchen. The men chiefly employ themselves in making forays upon weaker tribes or in hunting, the only home work they do is to build the house, to clear the land for cultivation and to help to gather the harvest. The curious custom among them is that when a man through cowardice or bodily incapacity is unable to do man's work, he is dressed in women's clothes and consorts and works with the women.

Marital Status: Marriage is a civil contract, that may be dissolved at the will of both parties and is celebrated only by feasting and dancing. Regarding the marital status, the women get full freedom in selecting her spouse according to her choice like 'Sita'in the Ramayana and 'Draupadi' in the Mahabharata. The Lushai women also get the chance of ' Sayamvara' marriage where more than one boy apply to win her consent and the boy when the girl selects, only gets the opportunity to become her husband. There is a particular social custom among them which is called ' Rim' where the young boys and girls mix freely with one another. In the evening the several boys come to a girls house and have evening tea with gossiping. It goes on for several weeks and months. The purpose of these evening party is to win the heart of the girl by the boys. Every boy gifts her ' bailo', a very special romantic token, and the girl announces her selection by putting one of the ' Bailos' on her hair and after that the parents of both the parties arrange the marriage for them.

Widow marriage is allowed but women do not often avail themselves of the privilege as a widowed mother is paramount in her son's house, Lt. Colonel Shakespeare wrote " if the man turns the woman out for no fault he must pay up her full price's as was the custom. The illegal child of a spinster gets recognition in the Lushai society.

Economic Status: The Lushai women have no rights of inheritance. The Lushais are patriarchal society and thereby the share of property goes to the sons. The youngest son gets the lion's share as it was said that the youngest will look after the parents. In case of no issue of sons, the daughter gets the property share. In case of polygamous husband, the son of the first wife will get the lion share than the sons of the second wife. The inheritance rule is different to the case of the Lushai's chief. The elder son only considered to be eligible for property.

The fast spread of education among the Lushais, both the girls and boys are getting educated and taking the Government'sbenefit for the tribal's qotas, the Govt jobs and other white colour profession are becoming very popular to them. This gives the Lushai women a chance to establish themselves for both economic status. The Jhum cultivation is replaced by the orange cultivation with new scientific methods and many Lushai families of Jampai Hills are now on sound economic tract. Of course, the Jhum cultivation is the main occupation of mostly poor families. The residence of a powerful chief is generally surrounded by the houses of his slaves, who marry and cultivate lands enjoying undisturbed the fruits of their labour. On the death of a slave, however his wife and children and all his properly go the chief(Ref: Hunter ' A Statistical Account of Bengal)

The Religion: The Lushai are almost all Christians, "the impact of Christianity on the Lushai people of Tripura is great" says A. M. Dutta, a scholar made his research on the Lushais of Jampai Hills in Tripura. In census of 1931 out of 2175 Lushai of Tripura, 2102 people were recorded as Christians. Only 73 persons remaining non Christians. With march of time, the entire Lushai people of Tripura embraced Christianity.

The Lushai Christian get food, clothes and medicines from the Christian Church authorities of New Zealand on the occasion of big festivals. For higher education, the Lushai go to New Zealand, Shillong, Aiwzal, etc where they study in the medium of English even when reading in a school or college of Tripura. This is due to their Christianity and missionary influence. Even Lushai Christian family perform baptism of these boys and girls at the age of fifteen (Ref: Dr. Dwijendra Lal Bhowmik Tribal Religion of Tripura-page 58-59). The Lushais have no distinctions of caste, they all eat together and each man is on an equality with the others. But as all other tribal groups, the religious rituals are performed by man head priest and women are simple carrier and stand by coordination to comply orders and arrangement according to their head priest.

If we look to the recorded facts about the tribal life of Tripura in Hunter, Lewin, or Hutchinston's authentic books, we find almost the same observations. But after more than hundred year, a gentle breeze of change has been blowing in almost every field of the Tribal life. Education, occupational mobility and government service usher in a new lease of life in their traditional society based on gathering and shifting cultivation. Marriage by elopement, or by service or by paying bride price are now almost a thing of past. Now a bridal skill has not been measured on her weaving skill but her educational achievement with given economic package.

Empowerment and Tribal Women: A Bird's Eye View

Smt. Karabi Debbarma, a noted coloumnist & the ex- Principal of the Women's College, Agartala {an interview with her thoughtful views & rich experiences has been given in the questionnaire section on some leading tribal women of Tripura } in her 'Prabanda Sangraha', cited two important quotations to discuss the value of education in a tribal women's life of Tripura. The editor of the Godays Ladies, an American women's magagine, wrote "To ensure good mothers there must be the means of a good education provided for young girls. Better leave the boy of generation without learning than the girls if one sex must be doomed to ignorance"

The other one is from our own homeland's greatest ever woman's idea - the late Prime Minister of India, Smt. Indira Gandhi- "The education of women is even more important than the education of men because each educated women influence the young generation and society in a very special way".

Swami Vivekananda, Iswar Chandra Vidhyasagar, Raja Rammohan Roy are those few great souls who brought forth this truth against many social odds. That was the beginning and through the wings of time, their golden efforts spread fruitful result more or less to every section of society. Like rain water, the upper section of society which got the water drops of education first to make themselves prosperous pass the next drops underneath. Thus the women in general and tribal women in particular, are coming out of the centuries old darkness of illiteracy & ignorance, though lately but surely.

In a white sense, if empowerment means the freedom of buying & selling, dancing & drinking, the tribal women of Tripura enjoys those equally with their men. But in the freedom of speech, freedom of choice, freedom of taking decision, the tribal society also treated their women unequally. From customary laws to legal rights, in the past as well as today, she is deprived of both the woman right and human right. The tribal society can mend its wrong doing against woman whether it is rape or molestation by presenting a bottle of wine and a little amount of money to the Sardar of the community ignoring the fact that the victim remained in the dark with full disgrace and dishonour,

Many policies & schemes of the Govt. like forest reservation hit the economic condition of the tribal societies-thereby shaping their age old life model of jhum cultivators to plain land cultivators. For these new schemes, Jhum cultivation is fast becoming an almost non practicing occupation changing the portrait of tribal society in general and the tribal woman in particular.

The other sea changes along with occupational pattern in tribal women's life is the boon of education facilities which reflect its influence in their life style through marriage system, place of residence, family bonds, community organizations, housing pattern, cultural expression- a switch over for almost everything that ushers in a new meaning to tribal women's life.

Though the fact cannot be denied that the different advancement programmes of both the Govt & Non- Govt level spread the fruits of awareness almost on all fields, education at the epicenter sending its ripples encircling an alround development to the tribal society in general and tribal women in particular. At the same time, the traditional flow of culture and custom of the tribal communities are loosing its native fragrance under the influence of Christianity, Buddhism and Hinduism.

Some social evils so long unpracticed by the tribal society are creeping into tribal women's life and the newly introduced dowry system is one of them which is fast inflicting and debasing the marital status of the tribal women of Tripura. It is a great blow to the tribal women's social position. The hard, simple, uneducated life of tribal women is going to end to embrace the modern educated life with all its curses. The wound of transplantation made the tribal women stand on almost 'No man's Land'-loosing something for gaining something. She has lost her great skill of hard labour, freedom of pre-marital sexual life, honour of bride price, her esteem and pragmatism in home front. Leaving the value judgement comprising of morally wrong and socially undesirable over emotional overtone for tribal women's development, a scientific analysis shows us reality under sunshine. The age old concept of conservative tone that man, the superior gender must rule women as their inferior one is extremely hard to subside still today, both for tribal and non tribal societies. Therefore, the superficial observation about tribal women that the status of women in tribal societies is much better than that of women in non - tribal societies as far as the gender equation is concerned, is somehow mythical. The next one or two decades will disclose the real picture whether she is able to make herself empowered totally or partially-till then, let us cross our fingers.

4
Conclusion

Women in every community and every society constitute half of the population but what is called women's question is not a question of the half only, it is ultimately the question of the entire community and entire society. Thus any society or community cannot move forward without considering half of its body, the women.

So the women's question cannot be considered separately and divorced from the concern of the menfolk. And in considering the women question, every society and every community has to draw women from their untoward condition into a congenial one. Regarding women's status and empowerment movement some basic points should be remembered at the root level on three fields particularly social development, educational development and economic development.

We have already analysed the status and empowerment of the women of nine major tribal communities of Tripura depending on these three basic points. It is found that all the four tribal societies are not egalitarian in pattern. Though the Tribal women's participation in almost all fields of life is equal but their positions and authorities are limited. This discrimination is more acute in remotest rural areas as the urban tribal women have been able to overcome both their backwardness and also rural disadvantages. The achievements of these minuscule sections of women cannot be regarded as a whole though this sometimes overshadows the negative sides of the total development of rural set up. Most of the Government programmes and private sectors work or any new NGO's attempts to do beneficial works for these backward communities go immediately to these already advanced section of the same community whereas the backward and less advanced portion of the same community remain untouched from the fruits of achievement. It is due to the failure of some unbalanced and incomprehensive work programmes which are unable to reach the grass root level to help the genuine needy people.

So to draw out a whole community with maximum of its people benefited, specially the women section, a whole hearted multipurpose framework would be first chalked out to materialize with sincerity and honesty. Few suggestions can be drawn out to sent the results of development work rapidly and easily to the remotest angles.

1. In the rural areas, the scarcity of waters and firewoods are the two most essential things which handicap the tribal women's life as these kill both the time and physical labour equally. So the arrangement of proper drinking water in accessible distance with deep tubewells and the community bio gas system can remove some of the hardships of collecting firewoods and drawing water.
2. The government land reform measures should be implemented in such a way that the women members of the family can get equal opportunity to become the owner of the plot. Dispute regarding land alienation, a rational and scientific measure may be adopted to implement the Land Reform Act of 1960.
3. All the small scale government programmes and small scale cottage industries should be set up in

such away that the Tribal women can get chance to flourish their own ethnic items for which they have the first hand genuine knowledge and excellence. Under this sections, several handmade works like handlooms, poultry farms, knitting, tailoring should be developed with training and coaching to provide women with self earning.

4. Despite the govternment's effort to set up schools in almost all rural and inaccessible areas, the recent militant activities of some very few wrongly guided youfhs eat up the fruits of progress completely as most of these schools are now closed. A pragmatic approach with real sympathy should be made out on the part of both the government and also the local people of these area to get rid of this unwanted affliction. Thus all sorts of assurance should be provided to the teachers as well as students specially the tribal girls to get the benefits of the schools of these areas.
5. The fruits of development are most equitably distributed and effectively enjoyed only when development strategies are women centred. In poor tribal societies, women are at the centre of development needs and process.
6. Women are not a homogeneous group. And this is more true to Tripura's Tribal women as there are 19 different communities. There are many barriers that separate them but there are also some common areas that can bring them together. The process may be difficult and require great patience but it can be achieved.
7. It is important to trust local wisdom and give it a place in the development process. Different tribal women of different local area have considerable knowledge about their problems, needs and priorities and this kind of knowledge should be utilized in

planning and implementing development programmers. They may not express their knowledge methodically or scientifically for the lack of proper education but they have their experience which they explain through their own cultural codes. It is the possibility of development planners and activists to interpret codes.

8. For easy understanding of lessons imported in educational institution, mother tongue is the most important medium of instruction. Both the tribal men and women would be benefited immensely if such native tribal language be introduced.

The language problem creates misunderstanding in grasping the technique of education and teaching method. Kokbarak is not used by most of the teachers in the interior areas because the Bengali teachers as well as the Kokbarak teachers also do not take any interest in this respect. This is one of the reasons of dropouts. On account of language barrier the tribals suffer inferiority complex for free mixing with the non-tribals. The table below will show the drop out rates in Tripura and India.

Drop Out Rates in Tripura and India

Classes	*Sex*	*India General*	*S.C.*	*S.T.*	*Tripura General*	*S.C.*	*S.T.*
I-V	Boys	46.5	47.2	64.5	58.5	58.2	71.9
	Girls	50.3	55.0	70.2	59.8	63.1	76.5
	Total	48.1	50.3	66.7	59.3	60.5	73.9
I	Boys	61.0	65.1	79.4	74.1	75.9	85.9
	Girls	68.7	74.1	84.9	75.9	81.8	88.2
	Total	64.1	68.5	81.4	74.9	78.6	86.6
I-X	Boys	71.9	77.3	86.7	82.9	86.9	90.5
	Girls	78.3	85.1	90.9	84.5	90.2	93.2
	Total	74.5	80.2	88.2	83.6	88.4	91.6

Source: Annual Reports 1993-94, Ministry of Human Resource Development, Government of India.

From the above table it is clear that drop out for girls are always higher in Tripura than India. At the primary stage drop out was 48 per cent for general category, 50 per cent for S.C and 67 per cent for S.T. at the National level.

Dr. Satyadao Podder, Reader in History, Tripura University, Agartala in his Research paper entitled 'Education During post Accession Period and The Reangs' found that in 1931, the population of Reangs was 35,881 which increased to 84,003 in the year 1981, i.e., within the span of 50 years, their numerical strength doubled but their literacy rate has not improved to that extent.

9. For an effective monitoring machinery to ensure the implementation of protective legislation regarding work, urban culturally educated tribal women should come under one organisation alongwith the assistance of other unions.

   Late Jagat Jyoti Roy, Ex-Senior Auditor, A.G. Office, Tripura formerly a Research worker, in his article (Tui Vol. VII, July- Sept., 1999) 'Sociological efficacies for Industrial Development, suggested efficiency for industrial Development. Some of them are:

   (1) Abundance of forests, horticulture and mineral resources to feed, eco-friendly industrialization.

   (2) Key demographic indicator like literacy rate, sex ratio etc. are better than that of all India average.

   (3) Thriving trade activities within the religion and with the neighbour countries provide strategic market situations.

   (4) Strong traditional and Cottage industry base.

   (5) Per capita resource availability quite comfortable and high level of income with low productivity level.

(6) Possibility to cultivate Technological and Scientific skill among the man power.

It is found that about 74 per cent of the tribal population are living beyond the poverty line (Rs. 1100 per annum).

The following inefficacies for Industrialization are required to be overcome.

(a) Inadequacy of Infrastructural facilities.
(b) Restricted and Irregular supply of raw materials.
(c) Inadequate supply of power.
(d) Per capita consumption of Power (electricity) is 52.6 units as against the national average of 25.3 units. (1993-94)
(e) Due to poor finance and planning the State's Development is handicapped of Rs. 846.39 crores expenditure during 1993-94, only 7.35 of the resources fed from State's revenues. Total receipt from Central Government in the form of Grants-in-aid Loan is 70.60 per cent and 7.30 per cent respectively. And from N.E.C only 3 per cent per capita plan outlay under the Eighth Plan period, Tripura has it's outlay of Rs. 4099.00 while for any region Rs. 3348.00 all India average outlay during Eighth Plan s Rs. 5129.00 much higher than that of Tripura and any states.

Mr. M. Nagaraju, I.A.S., District Magistrate of South Tripura, in his Research paper "Empowerment of women: A case Study of Women Thrift groups under World Bank aided Rubber Project" (Ref: TUI Vol. VII 4th issue Oct-Dec. 1999) showed that the success of the WTGS in the project had a multiple effect among the tribal women of Tripura and as a result many organizations have formed WTGS in the state during the last two years. In fact now more WTGS are outside the project area than previously;

the other result of the success of WTGS is the recognition of womens role in making the rubber plantations a success.

The success of tribal women thrift groups in Tripura has forced us to reexamine the traditional perception about them. While they go un-chartered paths they provide beacon of hope to other members of their gender for their economic emancipation.

Mrs. Karabi Debbarman, Ex-Principal, Women's College, Agartala in her Research Paper Years of their indigenous Peoples and North East' suggested that

(1) There must be separate Ministry in the Centre for the N.E. region where the Ministry will be represented by one Minister, specially selected for the people from the N.E. region.
(2) The distribution of fund will not be based on population butbased on poor economy and backwardness of the state. No political influence should be entertained.
(3) Dialects as spoken by various ethnic groups of the region should be developed and education should be made available to their own mother tongue.
(4) Free flow of information of the day to day happenings of all the states of the areas be made available to the people through electronic as well as printed medias.
(5) In order to advancement of the regional economy of the general population facilities for marketing of their products should be made at National and International level.
(6) A feeling of brotherhood should exist to make everybody to feel as Indian.

Recently at the time of inauguration of a seminar organized at Gauhati by Nagaland Gandhi Ashram, former Chief Justice of India, Sri P.N. Bhagabati, urged the Centre to develop the communication Network in the North-Eastern region and eradicate the sense of alienation from the minds of the people on the priority basis.

Sri D.K. Tyagi, I.A.S., Commissioner, Government of Tripura in his research paper entitled 'Insurgency in North-East' (TUI, Vol. IV, 1996) concluded that the State's overall policy has been inconsistent and not directed to achieve the objective as laid out in the Tribal Panchsheel'. This concept seems to have gone under oblivian and, is not the guiding principle in designing schemes and programmes for the development of tribals. Such an attitude of the state has aggravated the tribal problems thereby resulting in upsurge of ethnic aspirations mainly due to a sense of alienation, deprivation and emerging political aspirations.

For development of tribal women in Tripura, we must bring all the tribals and non tribals with one economic framework with proper political socialization. In Soviet Union many tribal people have been fruitfully brought in line with other people but no attempt is being made even in present to bring the tribal people in line with the other people (Ref: The Momentum of Changes in the Life Patterns in the Tribals of Tripura by Dr. Suchintya Bhattacharjee, TUI, Vol. VII 4th issue Oct- Dec 1999).

10. Women's reservation within caste reservation must be ensured.

It also includes adult education, girl child nutritional programme, health education, income generating activities for tribal women, effectively raising age of marriage etc. But the dynamic of the women's movement is its meshing the young and the old, the pioneers and the new emerging leaders-strong second line must be groomed based on merit and leadership. Networks at the state and regional, at the village and the town level must be forged through increase in mass organization of working tribal women, in all level, low or high. The government should provide requisite financial assistance to the individual and voluntary efforts or organizations for carrying out their activities for tribal women of Tripura.

The Tribal Welfare Department, Govt. of Tripura, has taken various shcemes for the development of tribals which include 25 point Tribal Development package, Special coaching centres for class X failed, sponsoring of students to study outside the state, several allied programmes like computer training, multipurpose mechanic training, vocational training through school and other institutions etc.

For unemployed tribal girls and boys in different trades like watch repairing, electrical works, radio/ transitor mechanism, cycle repairing, masonery etc, a training course from 3 months to 6 months is being conducted by the State Govt. of Tripura through NBIRT in (i) Bisranganj H.S. School, (ii) Chandripara H.S. School, (iii) K.B.I. Radhakisorepur (iv) B.B.I. Dharmanager. An amount of Rs. 350/- per month is paid to every trainee. The Govt. of Tripura makes arrangement for loan to the trainees through DRDAs, S.T. Development Corporation for self employment, if they come out successful in the training programme.

The following photographs have been selected to show the development programmes of the Tribal Welfare Development, Govt. of Tripura, on the basis of Five years Achievements 93-94 to 1997-98 and four year achievements (1998-2002).

1. Watch Repairing Girls.
2. Electronic Gadgets Repairing.
3. Self Help group, Behalabari, Khowai.
4. Computer training.
5. Sponsored Students to Bharatia Vidya Bhavan, Allahabad.
6. Broiler scheme for women
7. Feeding centre under special Nutrition Programme.
8. Boarding House for S.T. Girls.
9. Distribution of Musical Instrument
10. Hon'ble T.W. Minister giving Merit Award to S.T. students.
11. Madhyamik failed S.T. Students.

Photo. 1. *Watch Repairing (Girls)*

Photo. 2. *Electronic Gadgets Repairing*

Photo. 3. *Self Helf Group, Behalabari, Khowai*
A Total amount of Rs. 910.00 laks was spent in the last 4 years for the Special Area Based Development Project.

Photo. 4.

Photo. 5. *Sponsored students to Bharatiya Vidya Bhavan, Allahabad*

Photo. 6. *Broiler Scheme for women*

Photo. 7. *Feeding Centre under Special Nutrition Programme*

Photo. 8. *Boarding House for Schedule Tribe Girls*

Photo. 9. *Distribution of Musical Instrument*

Photo. 10. *Hon'ble T.W. Minister giving Merit Award to a S.T. student.*

Photo. 11. *Students assembled before the newly constructed building for coaching Madhyamik failed tribal students of Kamalghat, West Tripura.*

A Report regarding the Progress of T.W.D. upto 31st July, 2002

Hon'ble Chief Minister, Govt. of Tripura, announced a 25-point Tribal Development Package on 26th January, 1999. This development package aimed at overall development of tribal dominated areas as well as the people of tribal communities of the State in listed items by 2002. This listed items covered education, economic development, infrastructure development, socio-cultural development and Health Service development. One Booklet containing the 25-target items in enclosed.

1. During last 3 years and a half, considerable progress has been achieved against most of the targets. A report showing the progress up to 31st July, 2002 is enclosed.
2. However, the major achievements under 25-point Tribal Development Package are as follows:
   (i) 434 nos. of Junior Basic Schools in ADC area have been provided with pucca buildings against the target 500 J.B. Schools, 216 nos. more school buildings are under construction and shall be complete by March 2003.

   (ii) 6 nos. of Residental School for Tribal students have been taken-up at Khumulwng, Ambassa, Kumarghat, Kanchanpur, Birchandra Manu, and Karbook, Residential School at Khumulwng has already been started with 65 tribal children and construction of Ambassa and Kanchanpur Resident Schools also are nearing completion.

   (iii) 4 nos. of college Hostels at Agartala, Udaipur, Kamalpur and Dharmanagar already constructed for tribal students.

   (iv) 8 nos. of Vocational Training Centres, against the target of 7 nos. are being run at Dharmanagar, Kulai, Tulasihar, Mandai, Bishramganj, Udaipur, Bagafa and Rupaichari.

(v) Special intensive Coaching Centres for Madhyamik drop out tribal students had been opened in all the four Districts. Out of total 4,442 drop-out students provided coaching, 2,187 passed the Madhyamik examination. The pass percentage is 49.23 per cent. This invovative new scheme was highly appreciated by Shri S.K. Nayak, Ex-Secretary, Ministry to Tribal Affairs during his visit to Tripura in March, 2002.

(vi) 15 Special Area Based Development Project have been taken up for comprehensive development of backward tribal areas. Special Project reports have been prepared by D.M.s and implementation already started. The main object is to provide basic infrastructure facilites like roads, electricity, irrigation and safe drinking water in the project areas.

(vii) Total 8049 Hact. irrigation potentials have been created in tribal areas against the target of 4000 Hect.

(viii) 1122 Tribal paras have been covered by way of providing safe drinking water sources.

(ix) 8 nos. new Primary Health Centres had been established in tribal areas and 4 more shall be opened shortly.

(x) Against the target of construction of 10,000 nos. dwelling houses, 23,460 nos. already constructed under IAY.

(xi) Construction work of one tribal Museum at Khumulwng is in good progress.

(xii) Old original names of 95 tribal villages rivers etc. have been revived.

Source: A Report by Shri Banamali Sinha, I.A.S., Secretary-cum-commissioner, T.W.D.

5

List of Gazetted Women (S.T.) Officers Among Four Major Tribes of Tripura

Sl. No.	*Name*	*Educational Qualification*	*Designation*	*Home town*
1.	Smt. Snehalata Debbarma	B.A.	Section Officer Tripura, Secretariat Service, Agartala.	Agartala
2.	Smt. Bhaswati Debbarma	H.S.	do	do
Agriculture				
3.	Smt. Alaka Debbarma	B.Sc.	A.O. Girania	do
4.	Miss Gitali Debbarma	do	A.O. Mohanpur	do
5.	Smt. Shyamali Debbarma	H.S.	Dept. of Horticulture	do
School Education				
6.	Smt. Jayasree Debbarma	M.A. B.Ed.	Joint Director	do
7.	Smt. Riva Debbarma	M.A.	H.M., Bodhjung Girls H.S.S.	do

(Contd....)

(Contd....)

Sl. No.	*Name*	*Educational Qualification*	*Designation*	*Home town*
8.	Smt. Sarojini Chakma	B.A. B.Ed.	H.M., Madhava Ch. H.S.S.	Mainama, Dhailai
9.	Smt. Jogomaya Chakma	M.A. B.Ed.	H.M., M.T.B.H.S.S.	Pecharthal
10.	Smt. Juthika Chakma	M.P.Ed	Superitendent/Phy. Edu.	Agartala
11.	Smt. Jumkabati Chakma	B.A. B.Ed.	H.M. (High) Chailengta Legunga High School Sadar	Pecharthal
12.	Smt. Bithikana Chakma	B.A. B.Ed.	H.M., A.D. High School	do
13.	Smt. Sulata Dewan	B.A. B.Ed.	H.M. (High) Ramguna Choudhury Para, Kanchanpur	Pecharthal
14.	Smt. Subrata Chakma	M.A. B.Ed.	A.N.M.Teliamura Maiganga H.S.S.	Teliamura
15.	Smt. Mina Chakma	B.A. (Hons) B.Ed.	H.M. Pecharthal H.S.S.	Pecharthal
16.	Smt. Kakali Chakma	M.A. B.Ed.	H.M. Badharghat High School	Agartala
17.	Smt. Shyamali Debbarma	M.A. B.Ed.	H.M. Nutannagar H.S.S.	Agartala

(Contd....)

(Contd....)

Sl. No.	*Name*	*Educational Qualification*	*Designation*	*Home town*
18.	Smt. Jaya Debbarma	M.A. B.Ed.	Lecturer Diet	do
19.	Smt. Anima Debbarma	M.A. B.Ed.	H.M. Bijoy Kr. Girls H.S.S.	do
20.	Smt. Prava Debbarma	M.A. B.Ed.	A.H.M. Harianandra Girls, Udaipur	Kamalghat
21.	Smt. Kalpana Debbarma	M.A. B.Ed.	A.H.M. Sonamura Girls H.S.	Agartala
22.	Smt. Kuheli Debbarma	B.A. (Hons) B.Ed.	A.H.M. Udaipur Girls H.S.S.	do
23.	Smt. Aparna Debbarma	B.A. B.Ed.	Tarapara High School	Agartala
24.	Smt. Namita Debbarma	B.A. B.Ed.	H.M. Barjala High School	do
25.	Smt. Manalika Debbarma	B.A. B.Ed.	Barjala High School	do
26.	Smt. Manisha Debbarma	B.A. B.Ed.	H.M. Lankamura High	do
27.	Smt. Manju Debbarma	B.A. B.Ed.	Rabikumar High, Sadar	do
28.	Smt. Rita Debbarma	B.A. B.Ed.	H.M. Khilpara High School	do

(Contd....)

(Contd....)

Sl. No.	Name	Educational Qualification	Designation	Home towm
29.	Smt. Chandi Debbarma	B.A. B.Ed.	H.M. Indranagar High	do
30.	Smt. Subhalaxmi Debbarma	B.A. B.Ed.	H.M. Kalaghachia High	do
31.	Smt. Namita Debbarma	B.A. B.Ed.	H.M. Tabaria High School	do
Higher Education				
32.	Smt. Manika Talukdar	M.A. B.Ed.	Joint Director	Agartala
33.	Smt. Sanchita Reang	M.A. M. Phil	Asstt Professor, Kamalghat Degree College	do
34.	Smt. Lpika Debbarma	M.A.	Asstt Prof. Kailashar College	do
35.	Smt. Sobha Debbarma	M.Sc.	At present, Inspector of College, Tripura University, Suryamaninagar.	Agartala
36.	Smt. Banani Debbarma	M.A.	At present Principal, Women's College Agartala, Tripura	do
37.	Smt. Manideepa Debbarma	M.Sc.	Principal, Netaji S.B. College	do

(Contd....)

(Contd....)

Sl. No.	*Name*	*Educational Qualification*	*Designation*	*Home town*
Other Departments				
38.	Smt. R. Debbarma	Madhyamik	A.R.O. Sadar, S.D.O.S. Office Khowai	Agartala
39.	Smt. Mithu Debbarma		S.D.C. Food Mohanpur	do
40.	Smt. Panchama Debbarma	S.F.	Asstt Employment Officer	do
41.	Smt. Bina Debbarma	H.S.	Finance Officer, Power Deptt.	do
42.	Smt. Binapani Debbarma	S.F.	Under Secretary State Govt. Secretariat	Agartala
43.	Smt. Ratna Debbarma		Administrative Officer Information Tourism Agartala	do
44.	Dr. (Mrs.) Panchali Debbarma	M.B.B.S.	Lady Medical Officer Central Jail, Agartala	do
45.	Smt. Chitra Debbarma		Under Secretary Revenue Deptt.	do
46.	Smt. Dipta Debbarma		Asstt Registrar, Co-operative Societies, Agartala	do

(Contd....)

(Contd...)

Sl. No.	Name	Educational Qualification	Designation	Home town
47.	Smt. Kanika Debbarma		P.S. IV, office of M.B.B. College, Under principal, M.B.B.C, Agartala.	do
Other Important Tribal Woman Personalities of Tripura				
1.	Smt. Karabi Debbarma	M.A.	Retired Principal Govt. Women's College Agartala	Agartala
2.	Smt. Bithika Debbarma		Ex-Member, T.P.S.C.	do
3.	Smt. Kartik Kanya Debbarma		She won the Assembly seat of Takarjala (ST) as a CPI (M) candidate and became state Minister, Deptt. of Social Welfare and Social Education Govt. of Tripura in 1993.	
4.	Smt. Basana Debbarma	M.A. B.Ed.	Retired H.M., M.T.B. Girls H.S.S. She was given Presidential Award in 1997.	Agartala
5.	Smt. Mangaleswari Debbarama		Vice Chairperson, Commission For Women, Agartala.	do

(Contd....)

(Contd....)

Sl. No.	Name	Educational Qualification	Designation	Home town
6.	Smt. Asima Debbarma		Retired Joint Director, Social Edu, Govt. of Tripura	do
7.	Smt. Anurupa Debbarma (Mukherjee)		Renowed Social worker and founder of Adivasi Mahila Samiti in 19 Member, First Women Commission. She was awarded the Tagore Literacy by Indian Education to propagate literacy among women. Also was the recipient of 'Mahabir Award' in 2000.	
8.	Santana Debbarma		She was given 'Kabir Award' in 1998.	
9.	Smt. Suniti Debbarma	B.A.	Ex. Major, N.C.C. Commissioned by the President of India Served as the C.O. of Tripura Girls' Bn N.C.C. Agartala.	
10.	Smt. Sandhya Rani D/B	M.L.A.	She won the Asharambari (ST) Khowai seat as a CPI (M) candidate in 1998.	
11.	Smt. Anjali Debbarma		Sabhadhipati, Dhalai Zilla Parisad, North Tripura	
12.	Smt. Jyotikanya D/B		Chairman, Kumarghat, Sadar	

(Contd....)

(Contd....)

Sl. No.	*Name*	*Educational Qualification*	*Designation*	*Home town*
13.	Smt. Manukanya D/B		Chairman, Ambassa Panchyat, North Tripura	
14.	Smt. Smiriti Rekha Chakma		She is the recipient of National Master Weavers Award in 2000 Dharmanagar, Masmara	
15.	Ms. Deva Bhakti Jamatia		She won about 20 medals for National meet as an Athlete, Called for Indo-Pakisthan meet.	
16.	Ms. Chaiti Debbarma		Crossed the Sea of Greece, in 1970 in the national school meet, and she got 4 medals. She set up a new record in Backstroke in swimming. For this, the journalists gave her the title 'Waterqueen'	
17.	Ms. Kaberi Debbarma		She got medal from national meet as a gymnast.	
18.	Ms. Nitmbini Jamatia, Ms. Jayanti Jamatia Ms. Jagatmani Jamatia, Ms. Nirbala Jamatia		All these ladies showed excellency in swimming.	

Bibliography

1. *Acharyya R.K.,* Inside into the Reangs.
2. *Bagchi Jasodhara,* Indian Women Myth and Reality.
3. *Bhowmik DR. D.L.,* Tribal Religion of Tripura—A Socio Religious Analysis.
4. *Bhattacharjee Kalyani (ed.),* Kichu Smriti Kichu Katha on Anurupa Mukherjee (Debbarma).
5. *Bhattacharjee Kalyani (ed.),* Mukti Andolane Bharatia Nari.
6. *Bhattacharjee DR, P.N.,* The Jamatis of Tripura.
7. *Chakraborty DR, T.,* Economic Participation of Rural Tribal Women of Tripura.
8. *Debbarma S.K.B.,* The Tribes of Tripura.
9. *Debbarma Suren,* Tripurar Adibasi, Jiban O Sanskriti.
10. *Debbarman Debapatiya,* Treatise on Traditional Social Institutions of the Tripuri Community.
11. *Devi Renu,* Women of Assam.
12. *Debbarma Somendra Chandra,* Tripurar Census Biborani 1340 T.E.
13. *Gupta Jayasree,* Human Rights and Working Women.
14. *Giri Mohini,* Emancipation and Empowerment of Women.
15. *Gon Chaudhury DR ConchanJagadish,* The Reangs of Tripura.
16. *Gon Chaudhury DR Jagadish,* Tripurar Itihas.
17. *Hunter W.W.,* A Statistical Account of Bengal Vol. VI.
18. *Hutchinson,* Chittagong Hill Tracts.
19. *Jamatia DR. K.B.,* The Jamatias of Tripura—A Historical Study (1863-1965).

20. *Kumari Ranjana (Edited)*, Women in Decision Making.
21. *Podder N (Edited)*, Prasanga Tripura.
22. *Roychoudhury DR N.R.*, Manikya Sasanaghin Tripurar Itihas.
23. *Roy Samiran (Edited)*, Taithyapanji O Nirdesika 2001.
24. *Singha Kailash Chandra*, Rajmala, Comilla, 1896.
25. *Singh J.P.*, Tribal Women and Development.
26. *Sen Kaliprasanna (Edited)*, Shri Rajmala Vol. I, II, III.
27. *Sahai Shrinath*, Women in Changing Society.
28. *Thorner Alice (Edited)*, Ideals, Images and Real Lives.

Magazine and Newspapers

1. The Eight First Amendment Bill, 1996 A Report of a Seminar held in Kolkata on February 2, 1997, Organized by Indian Association of Women's Studies, Jadavpur University, Kolkata.
2. TUI Vol. VII 2nd issue, April-June, 1999.
3. Satabarsha Saranika, Centenary, Publication of Maharani Tulsibati Girls' H.S. School, Agartala.
4. Tripura District Gazetters, Edited by K.D. Menon, I.A.S.
5. Raima, Special issue, December, 2001 Edited by Pannalal Roy, P.I.B., Agartala.
6. Raima- XI issue, P.I.B., Agartala- 2002.
7. Census of India 2001 , Series 17, Tripura Provisional Population Totals.

Newspapers

1. Employees Forum Vol. 23 , February, 2001, published by All India State Govt. Employees Federation, New Delhi.
2. Pranab Chatterjee, Sangrami Hatiar, February 10th issue, 2001.
3. The Dainik Sambad, 13. 07. 2001, Agartala Article of Acharya Dr. Dhayanesh Narayan Chakraborty, Bharatya Sanakritic Nari.

4. The Telegraph, Sunday - Women 12th November, 2000, 18th March, 2001, Kolkata 10th June, 2001.
5. Manabi - Saradiya, 1996 issue, Edited by Kalyani Bhattarcharjee.

Index

I

J

K

L

M

N

P

Q

R

S

T